Tan Malaka's *Naar de 'Republiek Indonesia'*:
A Translation and Commentary

Geoffrey C. Gunn

BADAK MERAH SEMESTA
2015

Tan Malaka's *Naar de 'Republiek Indonesia'*:
A Translation and Commentary

Copyright © 2015 Geoffrey C. Gunn
All rights reserved

Written by: Geoffrey C. Gunn
Re-typed by: Rossie Indira
Cover Design by: Rossie Indira and Andre Vltchek
Layout by: Rossie Indira
Geoffrey C. Gunn portrait photo by: Andre Vltchek

First published by:

The Research Institute of Southeast Asia, Faculty of Economics, Nagasaki University, Southeast Asia Studies Series, No. 38, 1996.

First edition, 2015

Published by PT. Badak Merah Semesta
Jl. Madrasah Azziyadah 16, Jakarta
http://badak-merah.weebly.com
email: badak.merah.press@gmail.com

ISBN: 978-602-70058-8-4

Tan Malaka Naar de 'Republiek Indonesia'

Geoffrey C. Gunn

PREFACE FOR THIS EDITION

As translator of Tan Malaka's work from bahasa into English I sought to redeem the Indonesian revolutionary's dream that his work could gain currency in a "world language." In similar fashion I am obliged to Badak Merah for "repatriating" this work back from China-Japan to Indonesia. This is timely, as never before for a younger generation of Indonesians growing up under the long Soeharto dictatorship, has the opportunity been presented to read modern Indonesian history objectively. It is encouraging for myself as well to view a number of fresh editions of Tan Malaka's classics reprinted in Indonesia, alongside translations of such other reference works as that of Harry A. Poeze, *Pergulatan Menuju Republik Tan Malaka, 1925-1945* (Jakarta, 1999). In this spirit I hope that this text helps to restore the figure of Tan Malaka to his deserved position at the centre of debates on modern Indonesian history. To be sure, as Tan Malaka sounded of the anti-colonial-anti-fascist movement and the need to overcome, no matter the hurdles encountered along the way, *"Padi tumbuh tak berisik* (rice grows soundlessly)."

Geoffrey Gunn,

Macau, China, March 2015.

CONTENTS

Preface for this Edition	v
Translator's Preface	xi
Life and Times of Tan Malaka	1
The Importance of this Work	3
Conversion to Bolshevism	6
Tan Malaka in Canton (late 1923-June 1925)	10
Tan Malaka's Return to Southeast Asia (July 1925)	11
Tan Malaka and the 1926-27 Rebellions	21
Tan Malaka in Bangkok (May-August 1927)	23
Tan Malaka in the Philippines (August 1927)	25

Tan Malaka in Hong Kong (September-October 1932)	26
Tan Malaka and the Republican Ideal	29
Tan Malaka and *Perjuangan*	35
Tan Malaka and *Diplomasi*	40
The Madiun Revolt and Aftermath	45
Tan Malaka in Indonesian History	51
Problems of Translation	55
Notes	57

Tan Malaka's *Naar de 'Republiek Indonesia'*

Introduction to Indonesian Edition,	5
Preface to Canton Edition	7
Clarification on Tokyo Edition	11
Introduction	15
Chapter 1, The World Situation	21
Chapter 2, The Situation in Indonesia	31
Chapter 3, Objectives of the PKI	39
National Program of the PKI	45
Short Clarification Concerning the Program	51

	Tactics and Strategy	59
	The Level of Offensive and Initiative	63
	Concentrating strength in an advantageous place and time	65
	Level of Consciousness, Will, and Discipline	70
	Strategic Blow	73
	The Indonesian Consultative Council	86
	Thunderbolt to clean the air	94
Notes		99
About the Translator,		105

Geoffrey C. Gunn

TRANSLATOR'S PREFACE

Originally published seventy years ago in Canton and Tokyo, this work by Tan Malaka, then Communist Third International Representative for Southeast Asia, found a sympathetic audience back in his native Indonesia. A trenchant critique of Dutch colonialism and call for revolution, *Naar de 'Republiek Indonesia'/Menudju Republik Indonesia*, may well have played its part in triggering the 1926-1927 communist uprisings in Java and Sumatra. Alarmed at the prospect of a premature revolution, Tan Malaka, from exile in the Philippines, sought to avert the showdown with Dutch colonial power. In the event the rebellions were crushed, the communist movement in Indonesia near decimated, and Tan Malaka in this text, found the Indonesian adrift, both physically and mentally. Physically, his life was, as he describes it, "three quarters life in jail", a reference to his arrest, imprisonment and banishment from the Dutch, British, and American colonies of Southeast Asia. Intellectually, Tan Malaka kept writing, but alienated from his former comrades, shifted to an arguably Fourth International or Trotskyist position. By the 1940s, at the time of his secret return to Indonesia, still under Japanese rule, Tan Malaka's Scarlet Pimpernel role, as much his "superhuman" reputation was well established among local youth. This mystique he exploited when dramatically, in August 1945, on the very eve of the Japanese surrender, Tan Malaka revealed his identity to the inner nationalist circle including Sukarno-Hatta and their Japanese military patrons (Admiral Maeda), and protégés, and staked his claim as revolutionary nationalist *primus inter pares*. But while Tan Malaka as midwife of the historic proclamation of independence could be tolerated, his vision of *perjuangan* or struggle brought him into irrevocable conflict with the moderates, especially around Soetan Sjahrir and Hatta. Not only did he disagree on the Republic's flawed military strategy – his analysis in *Naar de Republiek* served as vindication – but he fell out over the question of struggle versus diplomacy with the Dutch. In the fluid political environment up until a negotiated end to the independence of 1949, pro-Tan Malaka groups and parties burgeoned. Not even prison at the hands of the Republic could silence the now aging revolutionary. From the inside he launched a torrent of writings, political manifestos, and instructions to his followers. Threatened by the rise of old communist party, and in the face of a second rebellion, which erupted in 1948, Tan Malaka was given his liberty to help neutralize the new menace. More the irony that Tan Malaka was killed in mysterious circumstances by Republican forces in East Java in 1949, but in a familiar role, fighting. It could be said that while Tan Malaka was consumed by the revolution he ignited, his name and cause, even at half a century's remove, has not been forgotten inside or outside Indonesia.

As translator of this work into English, I have sought to fulfill what Tan Malaka regretted, namely his inability to reach an audience through what he called a "world language". Also, like Tan Malaka, I have chosen to relaunch this work in the land of the "geisha, beauty, and flower arrangement".

Geoffrey C. Gunn

Nagasaki 1995.

Geoffrey C. Gunn

LIFE AND TIMES OF TAN MALAKA

It is vitally important, twenty-five years after the consolidation and institutionalization of the Indonesian New Order regime of General Suharto, and fifty years after the proclamation of Indonesian independence by Sukarno/Hatta in August 1945, that Indonesian history, including "nationalist" history, be written from the outside. All the better that it be written on the inside, were it not for the powerful sway of state agencies – the censorship apparatus, official institutes of history and think-tanks – that have made a small industry out of rewriting modern Indonesian history in line with the Suharto-Army ascendancy. For obvious reasons such key events as those surrounding the coup of September 1965 and its bloody aftermath, are subject to major obfuscation inside Indonesia today.

Similarly, the full panoply of propaganda services has been brought into play to parlay the armed invasion and annexation of East Timor in 1975 into a "liberation". No less, as this work engages, the events of 1945-46 leading to the proclamation of the Republic, and its defence against armed colonial restoration (1945-49), are equally subject to official revisionism.

The role of Tan Malaka (1897-1949) in Indonesian nationalist history has always been provocative, just as the Sumatran-born former chairman of the Indonesian Communist Party (1921), subsequent Comintern representative for Southeast Asia (1923), and erstwhile "father" of the Indonesian nationalist revolution, has attracted the attention of a wide range of both Indonesian and non-Indonesian historians. [1]

In turn, Tan Malaka was a prolific author, penning besides his three-volume autobiography some scores of booklets and tracts, often written and published under great adversity. As Tan Malaka mentions in his autobiography, *Dari Pendjara ke Pendjara* (*From Prison to Prison*), actually written when imprisoned by his nationalist rivals, the work under review, *Naar de 'Republiek Indonesia'* (*Menudju Republik Indonesia or Towards an Indonesian Republic*), was "hurriedly" drafted in early 1924, while residing in Singapore. [2] But it was not until April 1925, during a period in Tan Malaka's life when he sojourned in Canton, that this Dutch language work was first published. A second edition appeared in Tokyo in December 1925 while another edition was also issued in Manila in the same year. [3]

The Importance of this Work

There is no question, however, that even if the outline of the work was first developed during Tan Malaka's stay in Singapore, the essence was developed during a long period of residence in revolutionary Canton where the young Indonesian, newly returned from Moscow as Comintern Agent for Southeast Asia, plunged into the ferment of the times. My translation is of a crude 1962 bahasa Indonesia typescript edition itself a translation from the Dutch original.

It is not sure how many copies of this book arrived back in the Dutch East Indies in the year between its publication and the rebellions, but British archival sources reveal that "a large number" of newly printed copies of *Naar de 'Republiek Indonesia'* were discovered in December 1926 at 46 Clyde Street Singapore, residence of one Agam Puteh, a known communist sympathizer. [4] This is not surprising as the colonial port city at various times in the late 1920s and early 1930s hosted numerous among the Indonesian exiles, including members of the exiled Central Committee. Both Tan Malaka and Djamaluddin Tanin, a committee member, confirm that copies of the work were sent to Mohamad Hatta and Sukarno, the future co-proclaimers of Indonesian independence from Dutch colonialism.

It can be said that the importance of this work, written when Tan Malaka was twenty-eight years old, lies not only in the force of ideas it sets down on the political economy of the East Indies, but also in its trenchant analysis of the crisis of capitalism, notably, the contradiction between the colonial and imperial powers and the prophecy of world war. But, as work of praxis in the Leninist tradition, it also stood as a clarion call for the revolution led locally by the Indonesian Communist Party or PKI. It also sets down specific guidelines as to insurrectionary tactics, bearing upon the real situation confronted by the Republic in the face of British and Dutch counter-revolutionary violence after the Japanese surrender in August 1945. Nevertheless, at the time of writing this work, Tan Malaka did not consider a general uprising in the Dutch East Indies propitious. Rather, he counseled, revolutionary activities should be limited for the time being to local strikes and actions.

As text, to whom was this work addressed? In part, Tan Malaka answers this question himself, the Dutch educated intelligentsia of the Dutch East Indies, the products of the "ethical" policy he attacks.

The question might also be raised as to how far this tract by Tan Malaka, in his capacity of Comintern representative of the PKI, went to encouraging the abortive 1926-27 rebellions in Sumatra and Java, notwithstanding reservations expressed by the Indonesian revolutionary to the central committee in exile in Singapore?

According to an official Dutch report[5] on the rebellion in west Sumatra, some people were "more or less" acquainted with Tan Malaka's *Naar de 'Republiek Indonesia'* which had been partly translated into Malay, mimeographed, and sent out to party sections by the PKI central committee. It is also true that certain of the themes raised by Tan Malaka in this work had been replayed in other texts written during approximately the same period. The Dutch report, for example, considered *Naar de Republiek* as "to a large extent" identical with his *Semangat-Moeda De Jonge Geest* [The Young Spirit], published in Tokyo in January 1926. A work of Marxist exegesis, also compared in the Dutch report to the Indian Marxist Roy's *La Liberation des Indes*, the question might also be asked as to what contribution this slim volume made to the course of modern Indonesian history?

Conversion to Bolshevism

It is important to set the text of this book against Tan Malaka's own life and times, for he was thrice imprisoned and banished by three colonial powers in Asia. First, he was arrested and briefly imprisoned by the Dutch authorities prior to banishment from his native Indonesia in mid-1922 for alleged various revolutionary activities. Second, he was arrested in August 1927 by the American authorities in the Philippines and subsequently banished. Third, in 1932, he was arrested by the British authorities in Hong Kong, imprisoned and likewise banished. As Tan Malaka has himself written, in the last two cases the countries concerned had broken with their political traditions by denying him the right of asylum. [6]

Born in 1896, Tan Malaka was the son of a high official in the Minangkabau region of Sumatra. 1917, the year of the Bolshevik revolution, found him in Holland, where for six years, he continued his schooling. Attracted by the tumultuous events unfolding in Russia, and having broken with his patrician Dutch sponsor, he traveled to Moscow where for several months he absorbed at first hand the lessons of the revolution. Thus armed, he returned to the Indies (November 1919), found employment as a supervisor of schools for the children of plantation coolies in the Deli region of Sumatra, but also helped form the Indonesian Communist Party (PKI), the Sarekat Islam (SI), and communist schools. Moving on to Java, where he set about organizing a school in Semarang, Tan Malaka was elevated, at the age of twenty-five, to the chairmanship of the PKI at its eighth congress in December 1921. But expelled from the East Indies in March 1922, after two months in prison, he proceeded to the Netherlands where he stood successfully for the Dutch Communist Party in the parliamentary elections of that year. Prevented by age from holding a parliamentary seat he then proceeded to Moscow via Germany to attend the Fourth Comintern Congress, arriving in October 1922 where he became an active Comintern organizer. [7]

As representative of the Communist Party of the Dutch East Indies (PKI) at the Moscow Congress, Tan Malaka came to attention for his critique of the blanket condemnation of Pan-Islamism as contained in the theses approved by the Second Congress of the Communist International, reflecting, intra alia, the Eurocentrist viewpoint among European Marxists, Lenin included. Tan Malaka argued with great force that this attitude had been taken up by bourgeois nationalists in the Dutch East Indies in order to isolate the Communists from the peasant masses: [8]

Pan-Islamism is a long story. First of all I will deal with our experiences in India (Indonesia), where we collaborate with the Islamists. We have in Java a very large union comprising many very poor peasants, viz., Sarekat Islam. Between 1912 and 1916 this union had one million members, perhaps it has three or even four million. It was a very large proletarian union, which sprang up spontaneously and was very revolutionary. Until 1920 we collaborated with this union. Our party, consisting of 13,000 members, went to the National Assembly and carried on propaganda. In 1921 we succeeded in making Sarekat Islam adopt our programme and it went into the villages agitating for the control of production and for the watchword: 'All power to the poor peasants and to the proletariat'. Thus, we carried on the same propaganda as our Communist Party, only sometimes under another name. However, a split occurred in 1921, owing to the tactless criticism of the leaders of Sarekat Islam. The government through its agents, made use of this split, and also of the decisions of the Second Congress of the Communist International, to fight against Pan-Islamism. The government agents said to the simple peasants that the Communists did not only want to create a spit among them, but also that they wanted to destroy their religion. This was too much for a simple Moslem peasant. The peasant thought to himself that he had already lost everything in this world ad that he was not willing to lose heaven as well. Such was the mood of agents made use of it. Thus we have a split." (Chair [Marchlewski]: "Your time is up") "I have come from India, it took me forty days to come here." (Applause) "The Sarekat

Islamists believe in our propaganda. They are with us 'with their stomachs" (to use a popular expression), but with their hearts they remain with the Sarekat Islam – with their heaven, which we cannot give them. Therefore they boycotted our meetings and we could not carry on propaganda any longer. [9]

As B. O'G Anderson has commented upon this intervention, throughout his life and often at odds with the Comintern, the Indonesian stressed the revolutionary potential of Islam in the colonized territories and the need for communist parties to cooperate with radical Islamic groups. [10] Yet, as mentioned below, Tan Malaka was also prepared to change his mind on that question, especially as he came to know better the concrete situation in colonial Malaya and Singapore. In any case, whatever the mixed reception in Moscow, the Indonesian revolutionary was appointed Comintern Agent for Southeast Asia at the Executive Committee of the Comintern International (ECCI) plenum of June 1923.

Tan Malaka in Canton
(late 1923-June 1925)

Following his new appointment, Tan Malaka set up headquarters in Canton arriving in the southern Chinese city in mid to late 1923. There he plunged into the demi-monde of underground Comintern work, especially on labour issues, which brought him into contact with the leadership of the Kuomintang, including Dr. Sun Yat-sen, whom he met in December 1923, and also with a network of agents which linked the bustling river port city with the revolutionary anti-colonial stream in the British and French colonies. In his biography, Tan Malaka writes that discouragement, a sense of alienation in the Chinese city, and deteriorating health, obliged him to move to Manila in June 1925. [11] As mentioned, it was in Canton in April 1925 that Tan Malaka first published *Naar de 'Republiek Indonesia'*.

What was the situation in Canton that helped shape Tan Malaka's thoughts? Under the control of Sun Ko, Sun Yat-sen's Western-trained son, Canton in 1923 was a quintessentially Chinese city in a modernizing phase. At least up until the boycott of general strike of 1925, Canton under the Kuomintang-Chinese Communist Party alliance experienced, in the words of one student of modern Cantonese history, a "remarkable expansion of commerce, industry and public services". Under Sun Yat-sen's protection, the city became a magnet for such future giants of the Chinese Communist party as Mao Tse Tung, who taught in the Peasant Training Institute in Canton, Chou En Lai who was political commissar in the Whampoa Military Academy where Lin Piao was a student, and Chiang Kai Shek was superintendent. From 1923, until the "White Terror" of 1927, Canton was the site of joint action in mass movements by peasants and labour groups. [12] The impression gained from a reading of Tan Malaka's autobiography confirms that these events deeply impressed themselves upon the young revolutionary, just as one can safely draw the inference that they influenced his intellectual and political development.

Tan Malaka's Return to Southeast Asia (July 1925)

Arriving in the Philippines in July 1925 in the guise of a returnee Filipino student, Tan Malaka immediately threw himself into revolutionary activity. There he made contact with a number of prominent Filipino nationalist leaders including

José Abad Santos and Manuel Quezon and labour leader Francisco Varona. Although not mentioned in Tan Malaka's autobiography it is also possible that he made contact with future Philippines communist leaders. Helen Jarvis, a Tan Malaka biographer, believes that it was Varona who helped him bring out the Manila edition of *Naar de 'Republiek Indonesia'* while Tan Malaka made himself useful as a correspondent on the nationalist newspaper *El Debate*. [13]

Anderson describes how in Manila, still as chairman of the party, Tan Malaka came into increasing conflict with his party comrades. In particular, he sought to heal the widening breach between the PKI and the old Sarekat Islam groups around Tjokroaminoto and Haji Agus Salim. He also warned of the dangers of sectarianism in a situation where the masses of the people were national-socialist rather than proletarian socialist in orientation. [14]

For the Indonesian revolutionaries-in-exile, Tan Malaka included, the colonial port city of Singapore provided perfect cover, especially the Arabo-Malay quarters of the city. As a British colony, Singapore – like Hong Kong – also allowed certain legal cover for banishees from other European colonialisms in Southeast Asia. Although the matter is not clear, Tan Malaka probably first visited or passed through Singapore in late 1925. In any case, at the age of twenty-nine he arrived back in Singapore in

May-June 1926 and, following another short absence from the colony, found employment as an office clerk in a German trading company. [15]

Among the first group of Indonesian communists drawn to the British police attention in the Straits Settlements since the foundation of the PKI in 1920, were probably Raden Semaun, who passed through in 1922, and Alimin, who stopped over briefly in 1924 en route to the Pan-Pacific Labour Conference held in June of that year in Canton. [16] Other known Javanese revolutionaries then sojourning in the bustling multiracial port city, included Musso, Winata, Boedisoejitro, Subakat, Djamaluddin Tamin, Sutan Djenain, Sardjono, Mohamed Sanoesi, Soegono, Sutan Said Ali, Abdul Ghaffar, and Sutan Perpatih. All became refugees in the British colony following the failure of the communist-inspired strikes in Semarang and Surabaya of 1925, or, in some cases, earlier. All made Singapore their base. [17] Some of this group like Alimin survived into the 1960s, or 1970s, in the case of Semaun. Others, like Musso, went done fighting in the Madiun rebellion in 1948. Others, like Tan Malaka were victims along the way. As revealed by a British report, the activities of this band of refugees and banishees from Java were not restricted to the Straits Settlements and the Netherlands East Indies, but also to Sarawak, and the Philippines as well. [18]

Locally, the Javanese exiles sought support and cover in typically Arabo-Malay sections of the port city. The first Javanese safe-houses described in British police reports was that of Sayid Mahdar at 84 Onan Road in Geylang. It also served as their postal address. Another was 709 North Bridge Road, then a house rented by Shaikh Abdullah Dahlan, the "ex-Sheikh-ul-Islam of Kedah". Addresses were a certain Tuan Moechter, and Haji Safie bin Haji Salleh,, a pilgrim broker who rented or sub-let the above-mentioned premises in North Bridge Road. The latter's father, a native of Semarang, had earlier been suspected of sheltering in his home four years prior the "notorious Javanese internationalist" and supposed author of the Banten revolution, Raden Semaun. [19] Sutan Perpatih, resided at 131 Arab Street, a pilgrim broker's establishment and also frequented 144 Arab Street, a Malay *songkok* (cap) shop managed by two Hajis. At least through to April 1926 the Onan Road address served as a regular meeting place for such conspirators as Winata Boedisojitro, and Sutan Perpatih. Most were under police surveillance. One of the proposals put forward by the Indonesians was to launch a Malay language newspaper in Singapore. [20]

It is possible that Tan Malaka made more than one furtive visit to Singapore during this period. British police records contain a letter written by Tan Malaka in Singapore on 6 November 1925, that is, seven months after the publication in Canton of *Naar de 'Republiek Indonesia'*. This was a letter addressed to

Boedisoejitro, then in Java. Contrary to his earlier optimism as to Islam, this letter baldly stated his convictions that the Malays of Malaya did not hold out too much revolutionary promise.

So far not the slightest advantage is to be seen from the work of our dealers (propagandists?) at (Singapore) or at (Penang). You may say that they are quite incapable, but in criticizing it must not be forgotten that the proper (indigenous?) inhabitants there, who form only a minority are all conservative in the manner of living and thinking and are petty bourgeois. On the departure of Hadji Moek from (Singapore) his kindness was invoked to make a visit to the Federated Malay States. The impressions which he obtained everywhere did not differ from those gained from (Singapore) and (Penang). The section of the people which understands (economy) and (politics) are the (Chinese). In the harbours, in buildings, in the trains, and above all in commerce, the (Chinese) are the most prominent. None the less their Federation is very weak.

You will understand that in these circumstances it is impossible for us to effect a union. The railway personnel and those in establishment connected with the railway are all Klings. In their circles no beginning has been made to set up any association. There is not a single daily paper in the Straits of Federated Malay States that is read by the Malays. In brief, if one looks for a movement in the FMS, it is not sought from the side of the Malays. It will certainly come from the Chinese and Klings, whatever sort of movement it may be. [21]

Perhaps, in this, Tan Malaka foresaw the problem of ethnic group competition in the revolutionary struggle in Malaya, competition that was bound to be unequal and weighted on the side of the Chinese and the Indians as he inferred in his letter. Nevertheless, membership of the first mass Indonesian nationalist organization, Sarekat Islam, and its adjunct *merah* or "red" inclined sections, also proliferated on the other side of the Malacca Straits.

As Yuji Suzuki has pointed out in an essay on the evolution of Tan Malaka's political thinking in the 1930s, the Indonesian became convinced that nothing but a mental transformation of the Indonesian people could break through the tautology of feudalism and imperialist oppression. As Tan Malaka wrote in *Massa Actie*, also penned and published in Singapore in 1926:

> You, 55,000,000 people of Indonesia, you will never become free and independent, as long as you do not throw all the dirt of magic out of your head, as long as you still hold to the ancient culture which is full of fallacies, resignation, and fossilized notions, and as long as you still have a slave mentality. You must unite all economic and social forces available to fight Western imperialism, which is well organized, but which is now in trouble; use as your weapon the revolutionary proletariat spirit, viz. dialectical

materialism. You should not play second fiddle [to] the Westerners in the field of analytical thinking. Admit in all honesty that you will and must learn from the Westerners. But you will not become the imitators of them. You must maintain yourselves as the man of wisdom in the East, who not only should solve the demands of their own world but also supersede the skills of Western precursors... Only when your society produces men who are better than a Darwin, a Newton, Marx or Lenin, can you be proud.

Suzuki comments on the above that, from individual liberation through the absorption of Western science, Tan Malaka inferred a progression to national liberation from Western domination, or from "ketimuran" to materialism, as he later expressed the matter. It is also important in this context to take note of Tan Malaka's lifelong avocation as teacher, a role to which he would return in the 1945-46 period when *pemuda* or youth became his favoured force in the struggles ahead. [22]

In this text, Tan Malaka also set down his ideas on the nature of Indonesian revolution and the course by which it should be advanced, as well as his concept of Aslia, a socialist federation of Southeast Asian countries and north Australia, an idea to which he would return in 1946.

Tan Malaka's scarlet pimpernel role was now well established, at least if colonial police records are to be believed. British colonial sources reveal that following one of his trips to

Singapore (via Penang?), he traveled to Thailand, by-passing Bangkok for Chiang Mai where he arrived on 24 September 1925. As the concerned Dutch intelligence operative noted at the time: "if Tan Malaka is established there, he can be up to no good..." Indeed, British reports hint that he established the "elements" of a communist organization in Chiang Mai, dangerously close to British Burma. [23]

In April 1926, Singapore emerged as the forum for a key conference of the exiled Javanese leaders of the PKI. In attendance were Alimin, Buditutjitro, Subakat, Winata and Musso. The idea of bringing together delegates from the Netherlands East Indies and various groups at Singapore was Tan Malaka's. he sought to temporarily transfer the PKI executive to Singapore and to reorganize the *Sarekat Rakyat* along the lines suggested in his writings, and, as endorsed by the Comintern Executive. Tan Malaka's concerns stemmed from his foreknowledge of the decisions brought down at the PKI Congress in Solo in Central Java (the Solo resolution), (actually convoked at Prambanan in December 1925 under the leadership of Alimin), to initiate strike actions the following May to be succeeded by a call to revolution in Sumatra and then Java. In response, Tan Malaka drew up a set of theses arguing the futility of such an adventurist course of action. He argued that the situation in 1926 did not meet the minimal condition of, first, iron discipline of the party, second, the broad acceptance by the Indonesian masses of the leadership of the PKI and, third, division among enemies at home and abroad. In this sense, Tan Malaka took a strong position against the adventurism implied by the call to putsch, small scale rebellion, and individual anarchism, as opposed to broad programme of education of the masses, strikes, boycotts and mass rebellion. The *Thesis* was passed on to Alimin with a view to having the matter discussed by PKI leaders in Java. [24]

Other members of the PKI remained in exile in Singapore where, as mentioned, the decision was made in Tan Malaka's absence – to launch the rebellion.

Tan Malaka, who vigorously opposed this foolish line of action, and, angered that the PKI leadership had tried to prevent the dissemination of his arguments, met with Alimin in Manila in February 1926, seeking the latter to return to Singapore, report his views, and influence the Party to reverse its stand. In the event, Alimin did not read Tan Malaka's theses at the Singapore conference, as agreed, and did not defend Tan Malaka's position that revolution under the present circumstances was not appropriate. Another member of the circle, Subakat, who concurred with Tan Malaka's point of view, was only informed about the thesis when he arrived in Singapore in June 1926. While Tan Malaka's strong reservations were registered by the PKI Central Committee, it had the effect of postponing, rather than countermanding, Musso's call for action.

But 6 May 1926 saw the Indonesian back again in Singapore. On this occasion, according to British police intelligence, Tan Malaka narrowly missed a rendezvous in Geylang Serai, the still characteristically Malay suburb of Singapore, with Alimin and his comrade, Musso, who departed for Moscow (via Canton) in search of arms. Only Subakat, the sole remaining PKI leader in Singapore, sided with Tan Malaka's view and together they worked to reverse the decision to promote the rebellion through the publication of pamphlets and the writing of letters.

After the news of the temporary postponement of the uprising had been received, the Padang Panjang (Sumatra) Sectional Committee directed an appeal to Tan Malaka in Singapore seeking his approval for insurrection without further delay. The letter was hand-delivered to Singapore on 10 September by a group including Zainun gelar Radja Marah from the Padang sub-section. Two days later, Tan Malaka called together his comrades in Singapore and repudiated Musso's call to action thus effectively countermanding the Solo resolution. It was resolved to establish a new Central Committee at Penang, headed by Tan Malaka. [26]

Tan Malaka and the 1926-27 Rebellions

The much discussed rebellions broke out in west Java in late 1926 and, in early 1927, on the west coast of Sumatra. In these actions, metal workers and dock workers struck in Surabaya supported by tram and railway workers. In Jakarta, pro-communist groups briefly seized the telegraph office. In west Java and Bandung, the Dutch pressed military units into action against communist forces. To some extent, vacillation among the party leadership helped the colonial authorities to crush the rebellions, facts not forgotten by Tan Malaka's adversaries. [27] In all, about 13,000 persons were arrested, about half of whom suffered imprisonment, many interned in the notorious Boven Digul prison camp in West Irian, from which they were not released until June 1943 ahead of a planned Allied attack against Japanese occupier.

Certain sections of colonial Dutch opinion tended to hive the blame for the rebellion onto the British for not deporting those Javanese revolutionaries who had through the years resided or passed through Singapore. This is a reference to two of the inner circle of Javanese revolutionaries, Musso and Alimin, who were arrested in Singapore on 18 December 1926 having arrived on the SS Deli the same day from Bangkok. For instance, as an article in the Dutch newspaper *Nieue Rotterdamsche Courant* of 28 December 1926, pointed out, the leaders of the revolt remained in close contact with the communist centres of Canton and Singapore. Further, the PKI leadership in residence in Singapore and the central committee of the party in Java, were practically indistinguishable. More damningly, it was alleged, the arms used by the rebels came from Singapore, and the banks which financed this traffic were also located in Singapore. [28]

As it happened, an official Dutch enquiry into the communist rebellion of 1926 in west Sumatra and west Java traced the "propaganda and criminal agitation" experienced in the Dutch colony to a "secret centre" in Singapore. This was described as a link between the PKI and the Comintern, between ECCI and the Profitern, between Indochina and the East Indies, between India and the Far East, and the meeting point between Chinese, Japanese, Australian, Indochinese, and Javanese communists. At the heart of this centre was alleged to be a eighty man secretariat divided into two sections, one concerned with propaganda, and the other, "direct action". [29]

The truth probably lied somewhere in between. In the event the British authorities in the Straits Settlements saw to a more active cooperation with their Dutch counterparts. As the British Consul in Batavia, Crosby, remarked, the Dutch were permitted to send special detectives including a European police officer to

Singapore. Together, the colonial police forces identified leaders of the movement, and intercepted and deciphered encoded correspondence between the leaders. Notwithstanding what Crosby described as "close and effective" cooperation, the British were not about to waive the law by surrendering up Alimin and Musso as strongly requested by the Netherlands' authorities. [30]

Tan Malaka in Bangkok (May-August 1927)

The years following the failed rebellion of 1926-27 in Java and Sumatra are described by Helen Jarvis, as the most shadowy of the revolutionary's career. [31]

As the West coast rebellion in Sumatra ran its course, Tan Malaka and Subakat departed Singapore for Bangkok, and, from this relative safe-base, tried to reassess the situation. Djamaluddin Tamin, however, remained in Singapore helping those communists who managed to escape from Indonesia and gathering information on the extent of the damage suffered by the party. In May 1927 he joined Tan Malaka and Subakat in Bangkok and, on the first day of the following month, the three established the Partai Republik Indonesia (PARI), a broad nationalist party. Djamaluddin Tamin subsequently returned to Singapore where he acted as PARI agent and kept up contact with PKI members until his arrest in 1932. Jarvis notes that several vain attempts to hold PARI congress were aborted. [32] While, as Tan Malaka wrote in his autobiography, the creation of PARI was not "an attempt to liquidate communism", [33] his plan was nevertheless rejected by Moscow as unorthodox and Trotskyist and he was obliged to resign his membership of ECCI. According to Jarvis, it is clear that Tan Malaka broke with the PKI and the Comintern in an endeavour to create "his own leftist tradition" [34] (arguably Trotskyist).

Meanwhile, offices of PARI were established in such Asian cities in Shanghai, Singapore, and Tokyo. While PARI continued to exist for the next ten years, at least a tenuous connecting link between the pre-1926 PKI and the Indonesian nationalist revolution of 1945, Tan Malaka appears to have distanced himself from the party following its foundation. [35] Two of Tan Malaka's underground PARI organizers in pre-war Java, Adam Malik, and Sukarni, however, would later emerge as staunch allies, after the 17 August 1945 proclamation of the Republic.

Tan Malaka in the Philippines (August 1927)

Shortly after founding PARI, Tan Malaka departed for the Philippines. Betrayed to the American authorities in the Philippines – many fingers point at the Dutch – Tan Malaka was summarily arrested on 12 August 1927. But the case backfired and Tan Malaka became a cause célèbre for local nationalists.[36]

Tan Malaka describes in his own words how he was soon bailed out of prison by Ramon Fernandez, an ex-Senator and ex-Mayor of the City of Manila and a "non-cooperator against American imperialism". Tan Malaka continues:

> The best lawyers of the Philippines under the leadership of the present secretary of Justice Mr. Jose Abad Santos offered me gratis their service. All the newspapers in the capital and provinces soon conducted extensive campaign for attaining the right of asylum.
> The Senate-president Manuel Quezon, declared that I am entitled to reside in the P.I. according to well established international usage... Mr. Manuel Roxas, president of the Philippine Legislature confirmed this declaration. The ex-President of the short-lived Philippine Republic General Emilio Aquinaldo gave a similar statement. The senators even decided to collect money on my behalf. The lawyers decided to fight my case to the finish, meaning to appeal to the supreme

court of the P.I. and U.S.A. in American Congress if necessary.

Even though, as Tan Malaka explains, the full weight of the American merchants backed by the American Army and Navy and, ultimately the acting Governor General, was ranged against this option, [37] eventually, by August 1931, he won his freedom in the form of a deportation order to China.

Tan Malaka in Hong Kong (September 1932-October 1932)

Having eluded the Dutch police who were awaiting his arrival in Amoy, the point of disembarkation, Tan Malaka moved to Shanghai. Apparently he met Alimin in the international port city in August 1931. But driven out of Shanghai by the Japanese attack of September 1932, Tan Malaka proceeded to Hong Kong where he arrived early the next month, together with a PARI comrade, Djaos, Tan Malaka was arrested on 10 October and interrogated by British officials from Singapore. [38] Although the only charge against him was illegal entry, he did not fight this issue, as Ho Chi Minh had done before him, but agreed to deportation to China in order to protect his local allies.

The arrest of Tan Malaka in Hong Kong was foreshadowed by the arrest in Singapore the preceding month by his comrade Djamaluddin Tamin and his circle of confidants. According to Tan Malaka's own admission, his earlier visit to Bangkok was to meet with the leaders of PARI to decide whether or not the time was ripe for direct action in the Netherlands East Indies. But PARI, he insisted, was a purely nationalist body concerned with rallying the Javanese and Sumatran proletariat to drive the Dutch from the Indies. He also denied the incriminating evidence contained in the papers of the arrested Comintern agent, Noulens, that he was charged by Moscow to proceed, along with Alimin, to Burma and foment revolution. Although the British had no proof, they found it hard to believe that an internationalist of Tan Malaka's caliber could not be implicated in subversive actions against the British empire:

> No direct proof has yet been obtained in the recent investigations of his present activities that Tan Malaka was being assisted by Moscow, but the overwhelming evidence of his history past and present, extending over a period of ten years, leaves little doubt that his visit South must have been connected with plans of wider import than the alleged localized aims of PARI, the leaders of which, it should be remembered, were recruited from the surviving leaders of the old *Partie Kommunist Indonesia* which engineered the 1926 rebellion in Java. [39]

As Tan Malaka wrote in his biography, such was British ambivalence towards this cosmopolitan native, that he was moved backwards and forwards between a European cell and a native cell. When granted permission to write a letter he took the opportunity to cable Lansbury, leader of the British Socialist Party. Secretly, he also sent a letter to independent Labour MP, James Maxton, and member of the British parliament. A second secret letter was sent to Manila and attracted a statement of support.[40]

Finally, on 27 October, Tan Malaka was informed by the British that an official Dutch case for extradition was not legally supportable and that he was to be allowed to leave Hong Kong. The choice of country was one that the revolutionary agonized over:

> It was most difficult choice in my revolutionary career… It was, as if I was facing a bridge of hair, over which the Muslim had to pass in the day of judgment, to reach the end, the heaven, where the hurris – the inferno I stand in the British gaol. At the end of the hair bridge was Shanghai, not with the big dove-like eyes of the hurries, but with the eagle-like eyes of the Settlements police.[41]

Even though his case was taken up in the British parliament by Maxton, Tan Malaka was deported to Shanghai. Clearly a skilled linguist after three years in China he traveled slowly back to Singapore, via Burma, where he settled in September 1937 masquerading as a Chinese and teaching school. [42] A witness to the Japanese invasion of Singapore, he continued in this employment until the middle of May 1942, when he was spirited across the Straits of Malacca to Medan in northern Sumatra with the help of his former Chinese students.

Tan Malaka and the Republican Ideal

Returning to the East Indies from Singapore in early 1942 Tan Malaka entered the final phase of his life, arguably also coinciding with the pinnacle of his revolutionary career. In the period up until independence was declared on 17 August 1945, Tan Malaka had already linked up with nationalist and revolutionary youth in Jakarta, including certain influential members of the nationalist leadership. Just whom he met among his circle, and, in what circumstances, remains obscure and the subject of much speculation. It is also clear that, while the left wing, including communist party organizations, remained dormant during the period of Japanese occupation, old networks were easily stirred by propaganda in the underground. The question of Tan Malaka's contacts with the Japanese is also at issue.

It is of more than passing interest that during

Tan Malaka's years in Singapore, up until his return to Indonesia still under Japanese rule, a series of novels appeared in Medan entitled *Patjar Merah Indonesia* (loosely titled "The Scarlet Pimpernel of Indonesia"). The characters of these stories, set in the 1930s, are Indonesian nationalists expatriated by Dutch colonial authorities who fought against the oppressive power of imperialism and Stalinism. The superhuman hero was widely believed to have been Tan Malaka. Such stories did much to add to the legendary aura of Tan Malaka and his shadowy life, and, prepared the way for his reception as a "superhuman" figure when he later returned to the public stage in the newly independent Republic. [43] While Tan Malaka learnt at first hand of the Tan Malaka myth – he writes of finding one such book in a Medan bookshop – objectively, he returned, as he acknowledged, as a "Rip Van Winkle", unrecognized and badly out of touch with local realities.

This reality, Tan Malaka discovered at first hand, following a hazardous journey across the island of Sumatra from Medan via Padang, Palembang, and Lampung to Jakarta, where he arrived in May 1942, renting a room in the mixed rural-urban Rawadjati quarter. Here, he eked out a bohemian existence writing what he considered his classic work, *Madalog*, and, half of the manuscript of another work called *Aslia*. In his autobiography Tan Malaka describes a rhythm of writing in the mornings, conversing with his working class *kampong* dwellers in the afternoons, and studying in the Gambir public library in the evenings. [44]

Now going by the name of Ilyas Hussein, and masquerading as an ex-clerk from Singapore, Tan Malaka got himself hired in late 1943 as a clerk in the Bajah Kozan, a coal mining enterprise in south Banten on the remote coast of west Java controlled by Sumitomo interests. This was no ordinary coal mine, however, but an example of what he described in his 1945 publication *Rentjana Ekonomi* as an example of "economic plunder" through the use of slave labour. In this position until mid-1945, when news of a Japanese capitulation gained increasing currency, Tan Malaka mediated between his Japanese military bosses, whom he evidently impressed with his energy and administrative skills, and the needs of the 10,000 or more *romusha* or indentured labourers, literally worked to death in the mine, and whose respect he also gained. As an example, he describes how he gained the confidence of other colleagues, as much the *romusha*, by scripting *sandiwara* or plays with historical themes, albeit loaded with appropriate and subtle anti-imperialist messages. [45]

There is no question, however, that Tan Malaka owed his position to the Japanese authorities, although that is not the same as saying that he collaborated with the Japanese as was definitely the case of Sukarno and Hatta. As Tan Malaka explains, such Japanese-fostered mass organizations as the Hokokai, the "Three A" movement, and Putera, touched all youth in Bajah Kozan. Tan Malaka explains, however, that in the local *pemuda* movement, two streams emerged. The former, the Angkatan Muda, with its focal point in Bandung, rejected Japanese promises of independence as improbable, and, the Jakarta-based Angkatan Baru, to which he sided, recognized that to actually win independence it was necessary to work with the Japanese and obtain it from within. To this end, Tan Malaka was chosen as local Banten delegate to represent the Aliran Baru at an upcoming conference in Jakarta aimed at forging a consensus between the two tendencies or at least finding sufficient middle ground for cooperation. In accepting the position, Tan Malaka is emphatic that he rejected any connection with the Hokokai (in which Sukarno and other members of the elite had been involved). But upon arrival in Jakarta, Tan Malaka was somewhat shattered to learn that the Japanese forbade the meet. Still going by the name of Hussein from Banten, he nevertheless used the occasion to forge key links with certain (unnamed) *pemuda*. [46] These contacts included Chairul Saleh, future Vice President under Sukarno, and Adam Malik, the enigmatic future Vice President of Indonesia under Suharto.

Meanwhile, on 14 August 1945, two days before the dropping of the atomic bomb on Hiroshima, Sukarno and Hatta returned from Saigon where they had extracted promises of independence from the Japanese Commander of the Southern Area. But, in the way of obtaining independence outside Japanese auspices, the two senior nationalist leaders were kidnapped by a group of *pemuda* whose loyalties lay with Tan Malaka, and whose number included Adam Malik, and Chairul Saleh. It is tempting to see the hand of Tan Malaka in this putsch but, equally, he saw advantage in working with his Japanese contacts, namely in the person of Dr. Achmad Subardjo, the Dutch-educated Indonesian advisor to the Japanese navy, and head of the Asrama Merdeka Indonesia under the sponsorship of Rear Admiral Tadashi Maeda, the "leftist" head of Japanese Naval Intelligence. It was Maeda who dispatched Subardjo to rescue Sukarno and Hatta from the *pemuda*. Thus, when the proclamation of independence was made by Sukarno and Hatta two days after the official Japanese surrender on 17 August 1945 in Maeda's Menteng residence, Tan Malaka, the *pemuda* groups, and, indeed, an outraged Japanese High Command, were presented with a fait accompli. [47]

While the matter is controversial, contemporary American sources reveal that, "according to documents that had come to light", Tan Malaka, "Father of the Republic", had a hand in this proclamation of independence, or, more accurately, a unilateral declaration of independence, and that he had urged Sukarno and Hatta to proclaim it without delay before the return of the Netherlands or the Allies.

This would explain the political will, signed by Soekarno and Hatta, and dated October 1st 1945, in which they stipulated that their power would be transferred to "Comrade Tan Malaka", should they themselves became incapacitated to continue the struggle for the independence of Indonesia. [48]

These basic facts are acknowledged in Tan Malaka's biography where he describes a meeting with Sukarno on this date at which the latter, now first President of the Indonesian Republic, assured him that, "if I am incapacitated [*tidak berdaja*], I would transfer the leadership of the Revolution to you". [49] Anderson confirms that, not only were the Maeda group informed as to Tan Malaka's whereabouts through Subardjo, later appointed Minister of Foreign Affairs in the first Sukarno cabinet, but, that, after 25 August, he moved in with the Subardjo family and was soon introduced to such prominent members of the Indonesian elite as Sukarno, Hatta, Sutan Sjahrir and others. [50]

As Tan Malaka wrote in his autobiography on the republican ideal:

> Forced by the people of Jakarta under the leadership of the pemuda headquartered at Menteng 31, on 17 August 1945 Sukarno and Hatta proclaimed the independence of Indonesia, and chose a republican form of government. To me this momentous event for the people of Indonesia meant stepping from the world of ideas to the world of reality in a period of little over

twenty years (I had written *Naar de 'Republiek Indonesia'* in January 1924 in Singapore). [51]

Tan Malaka's alienation from Sukarno's nationalist government became open, however, in November 1945 with the replacement of Subardjo by the moderate socialist Soetan Sjahrir, who, as prime minister, reserved to himself the position of foreign minister. It was on Sjahrir that the main task of negotiating the controversial Linggardjati Agreement (as discussed below) fell. For a short period, in June-July 1946, Sjahrir was abducted by Tan Malaka's supporters.

Tan Malaka and *Perjuangan*

From September 1945 to November 1946, the British command assumed responsibility for taking the Japanese surrender in Java, although widely believed by Republican forces to be a cover for a planned Dutch restoration. As witness of the conflict between the British forces and the people of Surabaya in November, Tan Malaka took a firm position in favour of the *perjuangan* or struggle line, as opposed to the *diplomasis* line represented by the Sjahrir government. To this end, in early 1946, Tan Malaka set about organizing a "Persatuan Perjuangan" (lit. "struggle front") but also going by the name of "People's Front", appealing to all revolutionary, nationalist, and republican groups. Dutch intelligence saw this move as a typical tactic of using nationalism as a guise for communist aims. [52]

As many as 133 parties, associations, and groups, joined the "People's Front", including Pesindo or "Pemuda Sosialis Indonesia", a party of extreme left wing socialist youth, and certain who formed into guerilla bands, who owed allegiance to Amir Sjarifuddin, then Minister of Information and later Defense Minister and Prime Minister of the Republic, in July 1947. It was also supported by the PKI under Mohammed Yusof, a figure who rose to prominence under Japanese sponsorship, not pre-war communist affiliation. [53] while the Labour Party (PBI), and Masjumi (the Muslim organization) also joined the People's Front, in March 1946, along with Pesindo, they withdrew to take up seats in Sjahrir's cabinet. Youth leaders, such as future New Order Vice President Adam Malik, and the radical nationalist intellectual Mohd. Yamin, were likewise attracted.

At the general meeting of the "People's Front" held on 4-5 January 1946, attended by General Soedirman, the Commander-in-chief of the Republican Army, Tan Malaka developed his "minimum program" around the slogans of "*Merdeka atau mati*" (freedom or death), and application of the policy of the "pointed bamboo". By this he urged rejections of all negotiating proposals tendered by the Netherlands, the withdrawal of Allied troops, and the recognition of Indonesian independence as a precondition for any negotiations. He also invoked the support of the Soviet Union on the principle of its opposition to any form of colonial rule. [54]

While Sukarno had addressed one of the People's Front meetings, it is clear that the Republican government began to view the growth of the People's Front movement with suspicion. The matter came to a head in February, when the People's Front demanded the resignation of the Sjahrir cabinet and adopted "an increasingly aggressive attitude". According to Dutch intelligence, the conflict then resolved itself into a struggle for power between Tan Malaka and the government in the person of Amir Sjarifuddin. At first, members of Pesindo were forbidden to attend the People's Front meetings, and then, Pesindo resigned as a body from that organization. Thus, by the time of the March 1946 meeting of the People's Front, only forty of the original political organizations were still affiliated with it. [55]

Now emboldened by its newly won support, the Republican government launched a countercoup, effectively preempting the emergence of a dominant socialist current in the nationalist revolution. On 17 March, Tan Malaka and other leaders of the Persatuan Perjuangan, including Subardjo, Sukarni, and Mohammed Yamin, were arrested by Republican troops on the pretext of leading Tan Malaka to a meeting with President Sukarno. They were subsequently interned – albeit not imprisoned – in an isolated village where they languished for long time. In a recent study the Indonesian writer, Aboe Bakar Loebis, claims to have knowledge which contradicts Tan Malaka's own assertion in *Dari Pendjara ke Pendjara* that he surrendered to Republican forces as he was promised a meeting in Yogya with Sukarno. Rather, he claims, Tan Malaka's arrest order was unconditional and actually ordered by Sukarno, not Sjahrir. [56]

In the same month, in shadowy circumstances, the Republican side moved against Mohd. Yusof, chairman of the PKI, and erstwhile ally of Tan Malaka. After his arrest, a special Republican committee was formed to purge the communist party of its revolutionary leftist-Trotskyist drift. While Yusof's PKI was repudiated as the legal successor of the old PKI of the 1920s, the "official PKI" was re-established under the chairmanship of Sardjono. A former PKI leader back in 1925, Sardjono had recently returned from Australia, where he had presided over the Central Committee for a Free Indonesia in Brisbane. Australia had been host during the war for 800 "Digulists", including veterans of the 1926-27 rebellions spirited out of West Irian in June 1943. With his return, a manifesto was issued proclaiming that the Party would fight for the maintenance and consolidation of the government of the Republic. [57]

The temporary relief on the part of the Dutch at the coup against Yusof's PKI, and the arrest by the government in the same month of Tan Malaka and followers is carried in the following, just as the sense of conspiracy is carried in general Western relief that Tan Malaka was – temporarily – out of the way:

> The danger of the domination of a Tan Malaka type of communist government was hereby averted. Soon the regular communist party, which had little or nothing to do with Tan Malaka's proposed *coup d'etat*, would make its bid for power in other and subtler ways".

> "Whether or not Tan Malaka will again play a role of any importance can only be proved by events. As the original sponsor of the Republic, as a veteran communist leader, and as a former, though renegade, disciple of Moscow, he will always command a certain prestige in some communist circles. [58]

In captivity, however, Tan Malaka proved as much an embarrassment to the Republic as on the outside. Not only did he produce a torrent of "prison writings" but plotted the kidnapping of Sutan Sjahrir, the Prime Minister, and Foreign Minister of the Republic. This was effected by Tan Malaka's protégés in the last week of June 1946, leading to Sukarno being presented with an ultimatum demanding Sjahrir and Sjarifuddin be dismissed and that Tan Malaka form the new government.

Increasingly, however, Sukarno came under mounting pressure from Tan Malaka's supporters to modify his position, notably in a demarche presented on 3 July 1946. This 3 July affair, as it was styled, was used, in turn, by the government as reason to continue Tan Malaka's imprisonment. On the other hand, Jarvis observes, the government was interested in developing an alternative left-wing pole to undermine the PKI around Musso, who had arrived back from Moscow in August 1948, and, whose position on diplomacy had become more hard line than the Gerakan Rakyat Revolusi (GRR) (as explained below). After two and a half years forced captivity, Tan Malaka was released on 16 September (1947), [59] some time prior to the outbreak of the Madiun revolt.

Tan Malaka and *Diplomasi*

In his aptly entitled autobiography, *Dari Pendjara ke Pendjara (From Prison to Prison)*, actually penned during this period of captivity, Tan Malaka reminds us that the Indonesian "*hari pahlawan*" (lit. heroes day), which commemorates the people's defense against the bloody British attack against Surabaya on 10 November 1945, was actually mounted at the head of the Bengawan-Solo valley, the location he targeted for the defense of the revolution in 1924. Notably, Tan Malaka deplored the attitude of Sukarno and Hatta, supported by Amir

Sjarifuddin, in resisting the actions of British forces in Surabaya and Magelang in September-October 1945. As vindication he cites *Naar de 'Republiek Indonesia'*. [60] There is no question that, from a reading of the text, Tan Malaka argues again and again the futility of making an armed stand in the large cities of Java and that some form of worker-peasant alliance based in the albeit densely populated East Javanese countryside would be the ideal site.

In fact, by time that British troops departed Java at the end of November 1946, some 55,000 Dutch troops had already landed, and, in the following months, by a combination of military and other methods including the deployment of economic blockades, the Dutch reestablished civil administration in Jakarta and other coastal cities of Java. Elsewhere in Indonesia, Dutch forces mounted a bloody "pacification". Against this background, a series of compromises were worked out known as the Linggardjati Agreement (drawn up before the departure of the British but not ratified until 23 March 1947). In essence, the Dutch recognized de facto republican control in Java, Madura, and Sumatra, while, at the same time, creating puppet states in the rest of the East Indies with a view to subordinating the Republic within a greater Netherlands-Indonesian Union. On 20 July 1947 – in the face of world opinion – Dutch forces launched an attack on Republican territory, the so-called first police action, in an attempt to restore the colonial status quo ante.

Tan Malaka also made his views on Sukarno clear in print. Described variously as "embodiment of all the bad qualities of Hindu-Javanese culture", non-revolutionary, opportunist, elitist, Sukarno clearly stood in opposition to the values Tan Malaka upheld, namely his "*kerakyatan*" or people-based, progressive and non-compromising anti-imperialist position. This criticism, not surprisingly, extended to the question of Sukarno's collaboration with the Japanese administration. As Mrazek observes, Tan Malaka's own non-collaboration became one of the most important values of his second return (even if it is true, as we have seen, that he had contacts with the Japanese Naval Liaison Office in Jakarta prior to the transfer of power). [61]

As the Dutch account points out, even after Tan Malaka's release from prison, remnants of his following carried on in the "Akoma" or "Angkatan Kommunis Muda", a communist youth organization, whose members were still faithful to the aging leader and who had never joined the official Communist Party. [62]

Meanwhile, in January 1948, an agreement called the Renville Agreement was brokered between the two sides on board a US warship of the same name. Under US pressure the Republic accepted the terms of the agreement, which left the Republic virtually, encircled by the Dutch. In part, PNI and Masyumi protest over the terms of Renville, led to the resignation of the signatory of the Agreement, Amir Sjarifuddin. Meanwhile, on

1 February 1948, Tan Malaka's supporters from the Persatuan Perjuangan established the Gerakan Revolusi Rakyat (GRR), as a front opposed to Renville with Tan Malaka as the spiritual head. Jarvis writes that one of the precipitating factors in the establishment of this front was the PKI's shift in line in 1948 from all-out support of Renville, and, in the Amir Sjarifuddin government, to opposition to the Hatta government that was implementing it. [63]

The GRR, in turn, was a merger of the following parties:
1. Partai Rakyat (People's Party of Maroeto Mitimihardjo)
2. Partai Rakyat Djelata (Common People's Party of St. Dawanis)
3. Permai, Persatuan Marhaen Indonesia (Indonesian Union of Proletariats)
4. Laskar Rakyat Djawa Barat (semi-military organization)
5. Persatuan Invaliden Indonesia (Indonesian Union of Disabled Soldiers)
6. Partai Buruh Merdeka (Independent Labor Party of Sjamsoe Harya Oedaja)
7. Partai Wanita Rakyat (Women's Organization)
8. Barisan Bantang Republik Indonesia (semi-military organization of Dr. Moewardi)
9. Angkatan Komunis Muda (Akoma, Youth-movement of Ibnu Parna)

Chairman of the GRR was Dr. Moewardi (kidnapped on 13 September 1948 at Solo),

Samsoe Harya Oedaja, Deputy Chairman and Chairul Saleh, Secretary-General. According to American sources, the objectives of the GRR became clear at its first meeting on 1 February 1948, where, an overwhelming majority urged, first, the seizure of power within a week's time, second, annulment of the Renville Agreement, third, formation of a revolutionary Cabinet with adequate representation of Tan Malaka's following and, fourth, implementation of the minimum program of Persatuan Perdjuangan (Tan Malaka's People's Front, which was dissolved in May 1946). [64]

The raison d'etre and aims of the GRR were further clarified by B. Siregar, who chaired a GRR meeting in Yogja. He clarified that as the GRR was a merger of anti-colonial parties based on the declaration of independence of 17 August 1945, it opposed negotiating with the Dutch [Linggardjati (November 1946), and Renville (January 1948) agreements], that consequently, it opposed the Hatta cabinet policy of compromise with the Dutch (as with the former Sayap Kiri or left-wing cabinet), and, that it sought to create a revolutionary government of the Indonesian Republic extending to the whole of the former Netherlands East Indies. [65]

In fact, while general meetings of the GRR were held in Djogja, Solo, Madiun, Kediri, and other places, the planned coup did not transpire and the GRR remained relatively inactive until August 1948. [66]

The Madiun Revolt and Aftermath

Meanwhile the communist leader, Musso, who had spent the war years in the Soviet Union, returned to Java in August 1948 under the guise of Soeparto. At a party meeting later that month he revealed his true identity, was elected party chairman, and joined the revolt which broke out in Madiun in early September. Musso, who refused to work with radical nationalists otherwise accused of Trotskyism, evinced both an uncompromising, albeit Stalinist, anti-bourgeois and anti-imperialist position. Musso's authority in a new PKI Politburo, nevertheless, was quickly accepted by Amir Sjarifuddin and other central and east Java members of the People's Democratic Front. Newer and younger figures rallying to Musso included the future PKI leadership group of D.N. Aidit (1923-65), M.H. Lukman (1920-65), Njoto (1925-65), and Sudisman (1920-68). [67]

The rift between the PKI around Musso and the American-backed or, at least, pro-Western Hatta government, reached crisis level on 11 September 1948 following a wave of disappearances of PKI officers in the Solo area. Lower echelon communist leaders in Madiun responded to this and moves by the Republican High Command to demobilize their forces, by storming the local Siliwangi Division barracks.

By 18 September, following an outbreak in fighting, pro-communist officers were in control of Madiun and surrounding towns. Musso and Sjarifuddin, who had gone over to the PKI, were thus presented with a fait accompli when they arrived in Madiun on that day. In the event, the Siliwangi Division under General Abdul Haris Nasution, crushed the so-called Madiun "soviet" within a month, leading to the death of Musso, bloody repression of the PKI, and the flight of remaining leadership. [68] Tan Malaka could have wryly noted that it was the second time in thirty years that Musso erred on the side of adventurism, exposing the party to destruction. Needless to say, the crushing of the PKI was met with relief on the part of the West, including the US, even if the communist set-back did not translate into immediate military advantage for the Dutch.

But this time, with the destruction of the PKI at Madiun in August 1948, Tan Malaka remained the foremost proponent of the *perjuangan* line. On 7 November 1948 various pro-Tan Malaka groups and parties established the Murba or Proletarian Party. Within a month Murba had attracted a membership of 80,000. The Party's minimum program announced late that month was based on the old Struggle Front and included, expropriation of Dutch property and armed opposition to the enemy. A maximum program charted a course towards a socialist Indonesia. Tan Malaka, for self-preservation among other reasons, departed in November for the Solo River Valley accompanied by thirty-five guerilla fighters. [69]

On December 1948, in the face of the long expected Dutch attack on the beleaguered Republican government seated in Yogja – the so-called Second Dutch police action – Tan Malaka went on the East Java service of Radio Republik Indonesia broadcasting a statement rejecting negotiation, such as pursued by Sjahrir and Hatta, and, compromise such as reflected in the Linggarjati Agreement and the Renville Agreement. As monitored and summarized by the local Republican delegation, Tan Malaka required his supporters and potential allies to:

1. Annul all inventions as Linggardjati, Renville and Hatta's aide memoire.
2. Root out all puppet states created by the Dutch with the help of their henchmen.
3. Recapture every patch of ground occupied by the enemy's troops.
4. Seize all foreign property
5. Restore self confidence and annihilate all fifth columnists.
6. Ignore all truce regulations
7. Reject any negotiations if not based on complete independence as proclaimed on August 17, 1945.
8. Unify all parties and fighting organisations and maintain the people's army.

US sources claim not to have been aware of Tan Malaka's whereabouts at this time except that he was known to be moving about the countryside "somewhere to the north and east of Solo". Earlier that month, the US Consul General in Batavia, Livengood, reported that Republican forces were closing in on "Tan Malaka Trotskyists" in the wake of arrest of Sjarifuddin and the leading communists. As evidence, he cites the closing of a Murba newspaper and a GRR radio license. [70]

As Livengood wrote prophetically on 6 December 1948:

> That the Communists have failed in their first postwar attempt most certainly does not mean that the Communist movement has been permanently broken.... The Communist group may have new leaders, Musso is reported to be dead; Alimin has surrendered or been captured; Sjarifuddin, Suripno, Daroesman, Djokosujono and, according to republican reports, even Sarjono have all been captured. Tan Malaka, who had been released from jail in September to split Musso's following, appeared to be the logical successor to leadership. It was thought that he would use the Gerakan Rakyat Revolusi (People's Revolutionary Movement) to rally the Left. The GRR published the daily newspaper Murba, and operated the radio station GRR. The former leader of the movement, Rustam Effendi, had been killed in the early stages of the revolt at Solo, so that Tan Malaka should have had little opposition in gaining control of the Left.
>
> But Tan Malaka has run into difficulty. Sjarifuddin and the last rebel leaders were captured on November 29th. Within 48 hours the Republic

announced that it was banning indefinitely the publication of Murba, suspending indefinitely the license of Radio GRR.
If Tan Malaka is in fact to rebuild the Communist structure, he will have to construct, first, new propaganda organs. What the strategy will be can be learned only by careful investigation in the Republic. But if the new Communist movement is to be truly a part of Stalin's international communism, it seems that the strategy will have to follow the International's Thesis on the national and Colonial Questions. [71]

In fact, such pessimism or apprehension by the US as to a communist revival in Indonesia based upon opposition to a colonial restoration tipped Washington in support of the Republic against the Dutch who launched her second "police action" in December 1948. In this military action, in the face of United Nations Good Offices Committee, the Dutch forces bombed Yogjakarta airport and captured Sukarno, Hatta, and several other Republican leaders. While the situation looked hopeless for the Republic, the Dutch troops soon found themselves facing armed guerilla resistance and civilian non-cooperation. It would not be until May 1949 that the two sides entered into negotiations leading to the Round Table Conference at The Hague, and the official transfer on 27 December 1949 of sovereignty of the former Netherlands East Indies to the new Republic of the United States of Indonesia.

Tan Malaka, however, would not live to celebrate this event. According to Republican sources, relayed by Livengood to Washington, in March 1949, Tan Malaka was believed to have moved from East Java back to Surakarta (Solo), his home base. "Republicans interpret this to mean that Tan Malaka has been unsuccessful in attempts to organize Trotskyist cells in East Java Republican Army units and may have returned to Surakarta to reorganize his activities". The same report confirmed that the Front Demokrasi Rakyat (FDR) was still active in Yogja-karta. [72]

On 1 April, as Livengood reported, Musso was killed in October by Republican armed forces (TNI) while Sjarifuddin was killed – read, executed – by Republican forces in Solo on 19 December. The same report signaled the presence of 2000 of Tan Malaka's troops in the Kediri area "not necessarily communist". [73]

In circumstances which are still fairly obscure, Tan Malaka was seized and summarily executed "most probably" on 19 February 1949 on the orders of the military governor of East Java. His corpse was never found. [74] Aboe Bakar Loebis, who concedes not to know who shot Tan Malaka, claims he was killed near Dewa Mojo beside the Sungai Brantas in East Java.

Tan Malaka in Indonesian History

While Tan Malaka was out of the picture, his ideals survived him in two forms, first, in the form of armed struggle, and second, in the form of parliamentari-anism.

With respect to the first, Tan Malaka's followers, organized as the Laskar Rakyat Jawa Barat (West Java People's Brigade), constituted the last sizable band of armed guerillas to resist the Republican leadership prior to their defeat in October 1949 in south Banten, and the capture of their leader, Chairul Saleh, in March the following year. In mid-November 1949, this group denounced the Republic's leadership and proclaimed itself as the Tentara Rakyat or People's Army to fight for independence outside of the United Nations Framework. [76]

With respect to the parliamentary or at least organizational struggle, the formation of Partai Murba or Proletarian Party in October 1948 just after the Madiun uprising was significant, according to historian Herb Feith, in the way it expressed "oppositionism" to participate in any cabinet, and, after the Round Table Conference Agreement, which it opposed, refused to recognize the "practical difficulty of governments". Nevertheless, according to Feith, Murba was able to breach a "radical nationalist appeal and a radical socialist one". Needless to say, Murba's inchoate Trotskyism and broad links with other parties, such as the PNI, brought it into conflict with the PKI orthodoxy. True to Tan Malaka's concept of armed struggle, it also forged links with the People's Army and "Bamboo Spear" organizations in West Java. [77]

How is Tan Malaka's role in modern Indonesian history perceived? As seen in official PKI historiography, the first four phases of growth of the Party since its founding on 23 May 1920 were; 1) the foundation of the Party and the Struggle against the First White Terror (1920-26); 2) twenty years underground and the anti-fascist front (1926-1945); 3) the August Revolution and the Struggle against the Second White Terror (1945-1951); 4) the broadening of the united front and the building of the Party (1951-). While, as seen, until killed in Java in February 1949 by a Republican soldier, Tan Malaka played a central and sometimes determining role in the first three of these phases, whether in situ in Indonesia, or, whether in exile, the PKI line is less charitable. In a 1958 publication, then Chairman of the PKI, D.N. Aidit, dismisses Tan Malaka's role in the November 1926-February 1927 revolts in Java and Sumatra. Looking back, he blamed the failure of the revolts on a vacillating party leadership, poor coordination, and the lack of resolute action once the revolt had broken out:

> More than that, he [Tan Malaka] and his clique openly adopted Trotskyite practices by setting up

a new party, the PARI (Partai Republic Indonesia) in a situation where the PKI was facing white terror from the colonial government and its lackeys.

All of this, he continues, made the work of the PKI more difficult and eased the divide and rule policies of the Dutch in mounting their repression. [78]

Curiously, perhaps, it was the first President of the Republic of Indonesia, Sukarno, who went out of his way to defend Tan Malaka and Partai Murba. By 1956, as Sukarno began to elaborate upon a form of "Guided Democracy", he increasingly looked to the 1945 generation of youth leaders, including Chaerul Saleh. Murba reciprocated. For example, in the course of an address to the Fifth Congress of Partai Murba in Bandung in December 1960, Sukarno described Partai Murba as "a revolutionary nationalist party of consequence", but also a party which concerned itself with social questions. On this occasion, Sukarno revealed that he had been acquainted with Tan Malaka, that he had read his writings, and had discussed them with him for hours. [79] In 1963 Tan Malaka was awarded the title of "National Hero" by Sukarno. For Sukarno, Tan Malaka was both a nationalist and a socialist.

It is of interest that Tan Malaka's role in Indonesian nationalist history has, paradoxically, been permitted some back-handed rehabilitation in the fading days of the New Order regime, albeit in the world of private letters outside of the state-controlled history institutes. For example, Aboe Bakar Loebis, writing in his 1992 book, *Kilas Balik Revolusi: Kenangan, Pelaku dan Saksi*, observed of Tan Malaka:

> Whatever his shortcomings and weaknesses, Tan Malaka was a brilliant nationalist fighter, thinker, and theoretician who developed and expounded progressive thinking far ahead of his time. Even among our modern nationalist revolutionary leaders, Tan Malaka was a giant. [80]

While Tan Malaka's "national communism", outside of the Stalinist tradition, came to be acknowledged inside Indonesia in the revolutionary period – indeed, we have shown him to be in the forefront of the revolutionary struggle – at the same time, his leftist tradition hostile to the capitalist underpinnings of the beneficiaries of the republican governments, makes him anathema to the heirs of that tradition, today in power in Jakarta.

*****

Problems of Translation

Where Tan Malaka himself complains of the surfeit of typos and malapropism in the Canton edition of this book, the problem was not entirely rectified in the 1962 bahasa Indonesia edition which I have translated. A crude typewritten and roneoed version published by Murba, the text at hand also suffers from typos, unreadable typeovers, ellipses, and curious usages not to be found in any dictionary. As a rule I have tended to sacrifice the bahasa Indonesia literary style where it inhibits a free flow of English. Stated another way, I have opted for fluency in English in the attempt to catch Tan Malaka's original meaning at the expense of a strictly colloquial rendering often made impossible owing to the above shortcomings. I have not had access to the original Dutch version or versions, nor am I aware of the existence of any such copies. I have, however, had the opportunity to consult a Japanese translation of the same Yayasan Massa manuscript from which I have worked. [81]

Notes

1. Rudolph Mrazek, "Tan Malaka: A Political Personality's Structure of Experience", *Indonesia*, No. 14, October 1972, pp.1-48; Harry A. Poeze, *Tan Malaka: Strijder Voor Indonesies Vrijheid Levensloop Van 1897 Tot 1945*, "S-Gravenhage Martinus Nijhoff, 1976; Yuji Suzuki, "Tan Malaka: Perantauan and the Power of Ideas", in L.Y. Andaya, C. Coppel, Y. Suzuki, People and Society in *Indonesia: A Bibliographical Approach*, Monash University, 1977, pp.31-50; Helen Jarvis (trans., ed., intro) *From Jail to Jail* by Tan Malaka, (3 vols.), Ohio University for International Studies, Monographs in International Studies, Southeast Asia Series, No. 83, Athens, Ohio, 1991.

2. Tan Malaka, *Dari Pendjara ke Pendjara*, Bahagian II, Pustaka Murba, Djogjakarta, nd. p.133

3. J. Th. P. Blumberger, *Le Communisme aux Indes Neerlandaises*, Editions du Monde Nouveau, Paris, 1927. Nevertheless, a search of major collections in Japan made by the author in 1995 did not bring to light any information concerning a Tokyo version of this book.

4. Public Record Office (PRO) Colonial Office (CO) file 273 MBPI, No. 46, December 1926.

5. *The Cause of the Communist Movement on the West Coast of Sumatra, Part One (Political Section), Report of the Investigating Committee Appointed Under the Government Degree of February 13, 1927*, No. 1a, Welevreded: State Printing House, 1928, in Harry J. Benda and Ruth J. McVey, *The Communist Uprisings of 1926-1927 in Indonesia: Key Documents*, Modern Indonesia Project, Southeast Asia Program, Cornell University, Ithaca, New York, 1960, p. 108.

6. Tan Malaka, "Letter to China League for Civil Rights", South America, February 1933 cited in Poeze, *Tan Malaka: Strijder Voor Indonesies...*, p.573.

7. Benedict R.O'G Anderson, *Java in a Time of Revolution*, Cornell University Press, Ithaca and London, 1972, pp.271-2 and see Helen Jarvis, "Tan Malaka: Revolutionary or Renegade?", *Bulletin of Concerned Asian Scholars*, 19-1, January-March, 1987, pp.44-45.

8. Fernando Claudin, *The Communist Movement: From Comintern to Cominform* (Part 1), Monthly Review Press, New York and London, 1975, p.258

9. *Bulletin of the Fourth Congress of the Communist International*, No. 7, pp.6-8 cited in Claudin, ibid., p.258n.

10. Anderson, *Java in a Time of Revolution...*, p.272.

11. *Dari Pendjara ke Pendjara* (Vol. I), pp.104-05.

12. Ezra Vogel, *Canton under Communism: Programs and Politics in a Provincial Capital, 1949-1968*, Harvard University Press, 1969, pp.33-4.

13. Jarvis, "Tan Malaka: Revolutionary or Renegade?"..., p.46.

14. Anderson, *Java in a Time of Revolution...*

15. *Dari Pendjara ke Pendjara* (Vol. II), pp.106.

16. cf. Yong Mun Cheong, "Indonesian Influence in the Development of Malay Nationalism, 1922-38", *Journal of the Historical Society*, July 1970, pp.5.

17. Various PRO CO 273 sources drawing upon colonial police records.

18. PRO CO 273 534, J. Crosby, "Notes on the Native Movement and the Political Situation in the Netherlands East Indies generally", Batavia, 26 March 1926.

19. PRO CO 273 534, " Political Intelligence", Singapore, 10 March 1926.

20. PRO CO 273 534, MBPI, No. 26, April 1926.

21. PRO CO 273 535, MBPI, 6 November 1925

22. Yuji Suzuki, "Tan Malaka's Mental Revolution: Development of Political Thinking in Indonesia in the 1930s", Jabatan Sejarah, Universiti Malaya, Kertas Seminar Jabatan, No. 7. The English translation of the passage from *Massa Actie* is taken from this paper.

23. PRO CO 273 533, J. Crosby, 28 November 1925.

24. Benda and McVey, *The Communist Uprisings*... pp.153-7.

25. cf. Jarvis, "Tan Malaka: Revolutionary or Renegade?"..., p.46-47.

26. Benda and McVey, *The Communist Uprisings*... pp.153-7.

27. On the uprisings, see ibid; and Ruth T. McVey, *The Rise of Indonesian Communism*, Cornell University Press, Ithaca, 1965, chapter 11, and George McTurnan Kahin, *Nationalism and Revolution in Indonesia*, Cornell University Press, Ithaca, 1952, pp.80-85.

28. PRO CO 273 535, "Granville", British Legation, The Hague, 4 January 1927.

29. Blumberger, *Le Communisme aux Indes Neerlandaises*..., p.72.

30. PRO CO 273 535, Crosby, Batavia, 7 and 16 February 1927.

31. Jarvis, "Tan Malaka: Revolutionary or Renegade?"..., p.46-47 and cf. McVey, *The Rise of Indonesian Communism...*, p.322.

32. Jarvis, ibid, pp.48-49.

33. Dari Pendjara ke Pendjara (Vol. II)..., pp.114.

34. Jarvis, "Tan Malaka: Revolutionary or Renegade?"..., p.49.

35. Ibid.

36. Ibid.

37. See Poeze, *Tan Malaka: Strijder Voor Indonesies...*, pp.362-80 for very detailed analysis of official and press accounts relating to the Manila trial and its aftermath.

38. Ibid. and see Jarvis, "Tan Malaka: Revolutionary or Renegade?"..., p.49.

39. PRO CO 273 589 13040 1933, "Rai Bhadur Prithvi Chand".

40. Dari Pendjara ke Pendjara..., pp.43-45.

41. Tan Malaka, letter, in Poeze, *Tan Malaka: Strijder Voor Indonesies...*

42. Dari Pendjara ke Pendjara (Vol II)... and Jarvis, "Tan Malaka: Revolutionary or Renegade?"..., p.51.

43. Noriaki Oshikawa, "Pantjar Merah Indonesia and Tan Malaka: A Popular Novel and a Revolutionary Legend", *Journal of Sophia Asian Studies*, No.4, 1986, p.1.

44. Dari Pendjara ke Pendjara (Vol II)..., pp.137-77.

45. Ibid.

46. Ibid.

47. See, eg.. Nugroho Notosusanto, *Tentara Peta Pada Jaman Pendudukan Jepang di Indonesia*, Penerbit PT. Gramedia, Jakarta, 1979.

Adam Malik stated that his first contact with Tan Malaka was on the night of 14 August 1945 but with a man going by the name of Husin from Banten (see Kahin, *Nationalism and Revolution in Indonesia*..., p.119.)

48. "Communism in Indonesia", compiled by the office of the Netherlands Representative to the Combined Chiefs of Staff, Washington DC, February 1946.

49. Tan Malaka, *From Jail to Jail*... (Vol. III. p.63).

50. Anderson, *Java in a Time of Revolution*..., pp.276-77.

51. *From Jail to Jail*... (Vol. III)..., p.55. See Anderson, *Java in a Time of Revolution*..., p.280, for discussion on the so-called Testament conspiracy.

52. "Communism in Indonesia...".

53. Ibid.

54. Ibid.

55. "Political Developments of the Communist Revolt in Indonesia", based on information compiled by Netherlands Intelligence sources.

56. Aboe Bakar Loebis, *Kilas Balik Revolusi: Kenangan, Pelaku dan Saksi*, UI Press, Jakarta, 1992.

57. US document dated 24 November 1948.

58. "Communism in Indonesia...".

59. Jarvis, "Tan Malaka: Revolutionary or Renegade?"..., p.53, and see footnote in Jarvis on Tan Malaka's publications in this period.

60. *Dari Pendjara ke Pendjara*..., pp.133.

61. Rudolph Mrazek, "Tan Malaka: A Political Personality's Structure of Experience", *Indonesia*, No. 14, October 1972, pp.1-48.

62. "Communism in Indonesia..." and, see Jarvis, "Tan Malaka: Revolutionary or Renegade?"..., p.54, writes that AKOMA retained a revolutionary approach up until 1965 when it was banned. In 1956

it was represented at the World Congress of the Fourth International by Ibnu Parna.

63. Jarvis, ibid., p.52.

64. US source: "Political Developments after the Communist revolution in Indonesia", based on information compiled by Netherlands Intelligence Sources, Annex: Gerakan Revolutie Rakjat.

65. Ibid.

66. "Political Developments after the Communist revolution in Indonesia".

67. M.C. Ricklefs, *A History of Modern Indonesia*, Macmillan, London, 1981.

68. See the judicious analysis of the Madiun revolt in Julie Southwood and Patrick Flanigan, *Indonesia, Law, Propaganda and Terror*, Zed Press, London, 1983, pp.26-30.

Sjariffudin, who had conducted the negotiations with the Dutch leading to the Renville agreement, had resigned the premiership on 23 January 1948 and launched a leftist campaign against the Dutch. He emerged as one of the leaders of the Madiun rebellion, prior to his arrest by Republican forces and subsequent execution.

69. Jarvis, "Tan Malaka: Revolutionary or Renegade?"..., p.53.

70. Livengood to Secretary of State, 2 December 1948.

71. Charles A. Livengood, American Consul General, Batavia, 6 December 1948, Subject: Indonesian Communist Party claims, No. 471.

72. Livengood to State, Batavia, 15 March 1949. Subject: Communist propaganda Opposition to republican negotiation with the Dutch.

73. Livengood to State, 1 April 1949, (incoming telegram).

74. Jarvis, "Tan Malaka: Revolutionary or

Renegade?"..., p.53 and cf. V. Thompson and A. Adloff, *The Left Wing in Southeast Asia*, William Sloane, New York, 1950, p.285.

75. Aboe Bakar Loebis, *Kilas Balik Revolusi...*, p.159.

76. cf. Ulf Sundhaussen, *The Road to Power: Indonesian Military Politics 1945-1967*, Oxford University Press, Kuala Lumpur, 1982, p.53.

77. Herbert Feith, *The Decline of Constitutional Democracy in Indonesia*, Cornell University Press, Cornell, 1962, pp.55, and see, pp.131-32.

78. D.N. Aidit, "The Birth and Growth of the Communist Party of Indonesia", in *The Selected Works of D.N. Aidit*, Vol. 1, Jajasan Pembaruan, Djakarta, 1959, JPRS, 6551, CSO 3477-D, p.283.

79. *Bung Karno tentang Partai Murba, Tan Malaka dan Perdjuangannja: Pidato Amanat Presiden Sukarno kepada Resepsi Pembukaan Kongres ke V Partai Murba di Bandung 15-17 Desember 1960.*

80. Aboe Bakar Loebis, *Kilas Balik Revolusi...*, p.159. Notable also, in this sense, is *Memperingati empat puluh empat tahun wafatnya pahlawan kemerdekaan nasional Tan Malaka*, Yayasan Massa, Jakarta, 1993. While I have not had a chance to consult this work, the "national hero" status accorded Tan Malaka by this festschrift collection, suggests that not all scholars inside Indonesia are bound to accept all the standardized official histories and historical verities on this epoch.

81. Hino Ryoichi, *Tai shu ko do: Indoneshia Kyowa Koku e no Michi: Tan Malaka*, Tokyo, 1975. This work offers, besides a translation of *Naar de Republiek*, a counterpart translation of *Massa Actie*. While obscure Indonesian terms are explained, the author offers no interpretation or elaboration upon the text.

Tan Malaka Naar de 'Republiek Indonesia'

Geoffrey C. Gunn

Tan Malaka Naar de 'Republiek Indonesia'

Geoffrey C. Gunn

Tan Malaka Naar de 'Republiek Indonesia'

Geoffrey C. Gunn

Naar de 'Republiek Indonesia'

TAN MALAKA

Translated by:
Geoffrey C. Gunn

Geoffrey C. Gunn

CONTENTS OF
NAAR DE 'REPUBLIEK INDONESIA'

Introduction to Indonesian Edition, 5
Preface to Canton Edition, 7
Clarification on Tokyo Edition, 11

Introduction, 15
Chapter 1, The World Situation, 21
Chapter 2, The Situation in Indonesia, 31
Chapter 3, Objectives of the PKI, 39
    National Program of the PKI, 45
    Short Clarification Concerning the Program, 51
    Tactics and Strategy, 59
    The Level of Offensive and Initiative, 63
    Concentrating strength in an advantageous place and time, 65

Level of Consciousness, Will, and Discipline, 70
Strategic Blow, 73
The Indonesian Consultative Council, 86
Thunderbolt to clean the air, 94

Notes, 99

INTRODUCTION TO THE INDONESIAN EDITION

Some time has passed since this publisher obtained the works of the late Tan Malaka, especially those printed and distributed abroad during the time of his expulsion from Indonesia by the Dutch colonial authorities. We are thus fortunate to have also received a copy of *Naar de 'Republik Indonesia'*.

The first edition appeared in Canton in April 1925. The second edition appeared in Tokyo in December 1925.

The book was deliberately written in Dutch for the benefit of Indonesian students in the hope that it would be well received and motivate them in their struggle for their country's independence.

The contents of this book offer clarification

on political matters and set down certain directives relating to the revolutionary struggle for the Indonesian Republic. If the sense of this book is that the PKI struggle demands the support of the student class it is because, at the time of writing, Tan Malaka was the Canton-based representative of the Comintern in the Far East.

We intend to popularize this book in Bahasa Indonesia as well as in other languages of the region to bring alive the aspirations and knowledge of a leader who became a victim on the way to realizing his goals.

It is hoped that this publication will serve to contextualize the revolutionary struggle in Indonesia as well as to serve Murba Party as well.

Jakarta, 1 January 1962, "Yayasan Massa"

PREFACE TO CANTON EDITION

"The birth of an idea can be compared with the birth of a child. It is preceded with the labour of the person who gave birth to it".

To our readers:

When originally published, this book was full of printing errors. Scattered throughout were words or sentences that would sound foreign to the ear of a native speaker of Dutch. The reasons for these errors are as follows:
1. This book was printed and corrected by a Chinese friend who had no grasp of Dutch language whatsoever.
2. The press lacked sufficient Latin typeface.

3. Finally, in three years of traveling around Asia, this writer has had no access to Dutch writings or newspapers and has not even been able to meet anybody who as much as understood this so-called "world language" in any form.

It is for this reasons, as much owing to small technical matters, that I have sought to draw the readers' attention.

I feel, moreover, that it is not necessary to pen an overly long brochure as this would reduce the passion and attention of the average Indonesian reader at the present time.

Now naturally, health permitting, I can proceed with my life which has been "three-quarters the law of the prison", "three-quarters life in jail", by moving to a country where I posses the full rights to live. But , having been refused by governments, I think for the meantime I must set aside hopes of returning to my homeland. Still, however, I do not want to be unemployed. I think I can better serve Party and people, especially, through making contacts with the students (intellectual) class, and by using this book as a tool.

Wherever are found sufficient revolutionary factors, and whenever, I surmise, attention begins to be paid to the revolutionary movement by intellectuals, then works like this will be for me simply like taking a rest. Certainly, this kind of work is more appropriate to this place, especially given the publication opportunities that exist in China. Working by "taking a rest" will sometimes be my means and my respected readers should prepare themselves to read even more books in the future.

To be sure, I will be preempted from executing activities like these should his Excellency the Governor General involve himself deeper in humanitarian activities. This is the opposite of what I can assume, because of health and exile. It is appropriate that I offer profound thanks to my Chinese fiends who have offered me as much assistance as possible.

Objectively speaking, I truly owe thanks to, or, that is to say, thanks to have been "necessitated" by Governor General Dirk Fock [1] who stimulated this small book.

Tan Malaka, Canton, April 1925

Geoffrey C. Gunn

CLARIFICATION ON TOKYO EDITION

We were concerned when we dispatched the Canton edition of this book to customers in Indonesia because of its less than beautiful appearance, otherwise offensive to the artistic sentiments of the intellectual literati who usually only read Dutch works.

But this is good for the intellectual awareness of our younger brothers as they are not small-minded about simple appearances. Numerous requests for this book show clear proof that we have won their hearts. This encourages us to reprint *Menudju Republik Indonesia*.

Even though police supervision is very strict in the land of the geisha, beauty, and flower arrangement, underground opportunities exist, namely a place where we can print this small book in attractive format with fewer spelling mistakes and malapropisms. This owes to the development of burgeoning workers' revolutionary movement.

In this preface we have already set down our apologies concerning problems with corrections and printing, even if they still exist in this new edition.

Our new readers can be informed of the difficulties we experience in improving upon our printing and proofing. With this we also want to demonstrate to our Indonesian readers that all acts to suppress our aspirations will be futile.

Furthermore, it is with a sense of satisfaction that, in commenting on the international and national situation, we have found no need in this edition to make any changes or additions. We have only found it necessary in this edition to add a new chapter to offer clarification on the idea of a *Permusjawaratan National* or National Assembly, while also setting down conditions and actions.

Furthermore, it is necessary to explain our opinions concerning students in other countries. Without doubt, students in China have proven themselves in the past to be more active than their Indonesian counterparts. Less than a month after our book went to press, more than 5000 students in China immediately left their school benches and joined in the strike actions and demonstrations by peasants and workers. [2]

On the national front the sickening attitude of

the "Indonesian fascists" causes us to hold our stomachs, even though they are falling over each other to a greater degree than we observed in the past.

Even so, we must gird ourselves against the enemy tactic of turning culture against us in the endeavour to eliminate the revolutionary movement of the Indonesian people, just as in the dark ages when village people would happily witness robbers struggling to free themselves from the hangman's noose. All of this just as if Louis XVI and Tsar Nicholas II had never lived.

History repeats itself.

It cannot be disputed that over the past few months the political struggle has sharpened political consciousness and the revolutionary activities of the Indonesian people of all strata have grown to an extent never witnessed before.

"*Padi tumbuh tak berisik* (rice grows soundlessly)"

Tokyo, December 1925

INTRODUCTION

With the utterance of "La etat c'est moi" the French Sun King acknowledged the meaning of the state in full consciousness. At this juncture the Indonesian Communist Party (PKI) can state that "the revolutionary movement is me". It is the intellectual faction with their familiarity with non-Indonesian languages who have this awareness, and who thus serve as the leader of all revolutionary peoples in Indonesia, and who encourage the popularization of the program and tactics to all sections of people.

The Indonesian Communist Party and the Sarekat Rakyat [3] embody the wishes of the revolutionary people in their struggle, having seriously shown their strength and understanding of the difficulties stemming from lack of revolutionary strength at that time. However, it is not our intention to refuse help from the intellectual classes. On the other hand, we acknowledge all help received with gratefulness, because they recognize our revolutionary basis. What motivates us to launch a special appeal towards the intellectual class who, at this time of crisis, otherwise raise questions on every occasion? On which side should one stand? As a leader of the revolutionary Indonesian people who has experienced the suffering of all people, we cannot marginalize the large or small social groups.

Dutch imperialism already worked to achieve this from afar. Accordingly, our small intellectual group, having reached a high status in the social and ideological fields, found that they could no longer make contact with the people. Being educated in a foreign language, they ruptured their link with the Indonesian masses, lost touch with the thoughts and aspirations of the people, and, accordingly, the ability to lead them.

We will provide you with a ladder so that you can descend to the people. It is not our intention to make Dutch the language of the people but only to provide you with the means to understand the people better than you have hitherto achieved through reading Dutch newspapers.

In every revolutionary movement the intellectuals play an important role. The core of the French revolution was shaped by the intellectual classes. In France, and other European countries, it was the students who assumed the role of leader of the bourgeois revolution in opposition to feudalism otherwise badly shaken up. The revolutionary movement, pioneered and led by revolutionary students, opposed the cruel authority of the Tsar. In colonial Egypt, British India, China, the Philippines, and elsewhere, it was the intellectuals schooled in imperialism who became leaders of the national movement.

Indonesia is no exception in this matter. Similarly, the first cry for national independence was heard in the high schools when they established Budi Utomo,[4] the people's organization and claimant for nationalism. However, while under colonialism, some students supported the banner of independence in the revolutionary movement while, over a long period, other students and intellectuals of Indonesia isolated themselves by adopting a passive and crass attitude.

Notwithstanding this attitude, the cry of the Indonesian masses becomes more urgent as time passes. Nevertheless, very few received help from the intellectual class but rather from the working classes, peasantry, and town dwellers. Through hard work they, too, can also create organizations even though those will in time attract the attention of the authorities.

Nevertheless, the work to create such an organization is not always smooth and easy. Because of the lack of awareness and experience of the Indonesian leadership, otherwise made more difficult by the Dutch politics of imperialism resulting in the expulsion of outspoken leaders from the country, it is very difficult for the Indonesian masses to create a revolutionary organization. It is this lack of awareness and experience, which caused even Budi Utomo to become "Party for people without hope". And it is because of this that the National Indische Partij[5] has been taken to the edge of the grave. Insufficient class-consciousness, organizational ability, and moral revolution are the main factors preventing an upsurge in work potential in the mass movement. Sarekat Islam becomes the prime mover of an aware mass revolutionary movement. The Indonesia Communist Party, Sarekat Rakyat,[6] and Workers Union, under their influence are all based on class consciousness, although, in the matter of organization and quality, do not fulfill our desires. Last year they demonstrated that they can resist the strongarm tactics of the reactionaries and, by so doing, have proven the way to life and growth. Merciless, narrow-minded, and reactionary Dutch imperialism has created a national and social opposition which does not permit peace, unlike even that in other colonized countries of Asia such as Egypt, India, and the Philippines, wherever the native peoples are given the possibility to improve their livelihood in the social and cultural fields. In Indonesia, the national authority (Dutch and Indonesians), are strengthened with class authority (capitalist and worker). In other colonized countries, wherever a strong element of national capital is found, national authority **is** not as strong as in Indonesia where 90 percent of the population live in poverty and suffering. Of course in other colonized countries a compromise exists between imperialist capital and national capital. Economic compromise is a reality and this leads to compromise between foreign colonizer and colonized. It would seem that in Indonesia there is absolutely no national capital with the possibility of creating an economic compromise, mainly because each demand on the part of the colonized to create a political compromise with the colonizer always fails.

You intellectuals must be aware that the Indonesian people, at least those who are objectively and subjectively revolutionary, will mark each political compromise with colonialism as a clear humiliation. Accordingly, if you wish to unfurl the flag of independence there is no other choice as firm and true as taking our side.

CHAPTER 1

THE WORLD SITUATION

From an economic perspective, the 1914-18 World War divided the world into two parts:

1. The defeated countries such as Germany, Austria, Hungary and Turkey. Also Russia, wherever the working class holds power in the economic field.

2. The countries which won the war, namely France, Italy, the United States, and others.

Soon after the end of the war, the defeated countries suffered greatly from shortages of food and manufactured goods, and capital and raw materials for industry. Additionally, the Versailles Agreement compelled Germany to pay up yearly to the Allied powers hundreds of thousands of gold marks in war reparations.

While countries such as France, England, and

Italy collectively won the war, they nevertheless also incurred shortages owing to huge outlays necessary to prosecute the war. Russia under the Bolsheviks inherited an empty treasury, a disordered transport system, and run-down agriculture and industry not much different than in the countries which lost the war. Only the possibility of rehabilitating the economy was far better than in the case of the losers especially as the Bolsheviks did not redeem debts incurred by the Tsar amounting to the sum of hundreds of millions. Over the past few years, however, we know that the money which has flowed from America to Europe has increased over time. The threat of economic crisis in Austria has already been staved off by Morgan, [7] one of the kings of capital in America. The Dawes Plan, [8] which commenced operation at the end of last year, has pledged a 800,000,000 gold mark loan to Germany. Not only the countries which won the war, but also those who lost, worked to obtain big loans from the kings of capital in America in order to recover from their economic crisis. Millions have been lent to Poland. According to the latest reports, France is already deliberating on a big loan. Many other countries seek to follow this example.

It is certain that Morgan would not object to lending money amounting to many millions if he was convinced that the capital would eventually be returned to his pocket three fold or more.

This conviction would soon be realized if

these loans were willingly and capably repaid with interest. A declining Austria has already become a half-colonized and economically dependent country and, because of it, certainly not capable of mounting a challenge. Germany, not trusted by the Allied countries, is now bound down. Germany has already obtained 800,000,000 gold marks in exchange for surrendering its economic, political and military independence. Germany has also become a semi-colony. In defeat, German militarism now survives under the soles of the feet of the Allies. The Allies now strive to contain the German military problem, identified by the former as large and of high quality.

This control extends to the spending and financial activities of the Allied countries in either directly or indirectly influencing income and circulation of German money. It is established fact that income acquired from taxation must be greater than circulation. The balance from income already removed from circulation must be transferred to the Allied countries. The National Bank, currently an influential bank in Germany, remains under the supervision of a board of Directors headed by an American. The German rail system, nerve centre of the modern economic life of the country, has already been internationalized, that is placed under the management and supervision of the countries who won the war.

The economic servitude suffered by Germany

is matched by political oppression, meaning that in both areas of domestic an international politics, Germany must bow to the wishes of the victors of the war. Only a government like that in Germany today can work within the Dawes Plan. The Dawes Plan not only guarantees the size of the payment of debt towards the Allied countries but also seeks to kill German industries and trade. Germany cannot be permitted to produce trading commodities better or cheaper than those of the Allies as was the case before the Great War (World War 1914-1918).

Because of the war, and because Germany lost all its colonized lands along with its markets for factory produce and sources of raw materials for factories, in addition to the liquidation or destruction of its merchant marine, it is extremely difficult for it to reconstruct its industry without external help, especially from America. On the other hand, at least for the moment, Germany does not appear to offer competition to the Allied countries in such colonies as Indonesia, and India, or in such semicolonized countries as China, Persia, and Turkey. Now we can state with clarity that the influence of America in these countries has been extensively developed.

The circulation of capital from rich countries like America to countries which either won or lost the war (Europe), and to semi-colonized countries (Asia), wherever capitalism is at an initial stage, and, wherever there remains a possibility of it developing more extensively, and while capital is allowed to circulate increasingly in countries that suffer shortages, raises questions of a revolutionary nature. "Is it possible that these years of crisis will be succeeded by a time of peace (*Pasifistische periode*), that is the peaceful development of capitalism as happened at the end of the last century?" (This would mean that the collapse of capitalism would not necessarily happen now but more likely within the next ten to twenty years).

We cannot answer the questions simply with a yes or now. It was along these lines that Trotsky clarified that the possibility of peace still exists. On the other hand, there exists sufficient basis to believe that capitalism will collapse. But, because there are hundreds of possibilities which variously confirm and defy prediction of a time of peace, we must never lose ourselves in such prognostications.

If we now draft up a political balance sheet, we can say that the possibility of success in dealing a blow against world capitalism is no better than during the initial years after the Russian Revolution in 1918-20. It is clear that at the present time we are in more of a defensive than offensive position. In October 1923, for example, we passed up the opportunity to strike and crush German power. Contrariwise, the German bourgeoisie later launched an attack against our party forcing us to work underground. Also in Italy, where fascist terror is still being exercised, our party must work underground. In England, where our party was still young, we finally obtained success after several years but (James) McDonald's Social Democrat Government was replaced by the Conservative Government under (Stanley) Baldwin. Whatever the working class does in the interim, it must retreat against reaction. In India, dependent in life and death upon British imperialism, the non-cooperation movement led by Gandhi between 1920-22, otherwise capable of rallying thousands of oppressed people to a single demonstration, has now become a passive parliamentary movement alongside the Swaraj Party.[9]

Weighed against the evidence suggesting a reign of peace, are certain developments threatening to crush such dreams of the pacific development of capitalism. One such force threatening to crush world capitalism is competition among various capitalist countries. Conflict between British and French capitalism is far deeper than what it appears on the surface.

It cannot be denied that economic and political conflict among two imperialist countries will lead to a new war. Germany, which has now become a half colonized and oppressed country, naturally hopes that it can utilize every good opportunity to free itself from the shackles that binds it. This opportunity can only be achieved if the unity between the Allied countries is broken through internal conflict. In the Far East as well, competition between different imperialisms sharpens. Japan, which feels itself threatened by the British-US alliance, has already fallen into the embrace of its foremost enemy, the Soviet Union. [10] Conflict between capitalist countries, both within Europe as well as in Asian markets, habitually raise up the prospects of world war. The construction of the naval base in Singapore by the British Conservative government not only illustrates the state of war preparations going on in the Pacific Ocean but reveals the growing cooperation between the American, British, and Dutch navies in preparing for the eventuality of a war between America and Japan. The hasty development of the Army and Navy in Japan all serve to strengthen our assumption of the recurrence of a world war in the Pacific, even more terrible than the last war.

The moving force behind impending war – imperialist war – is national rivalry among various capitalist countries in the world, and not national conflict as such. The development of capitalism carries the seeds of irreconcilable conflict between the bourgeoisie and the working class. Class struggle will both bring down the capitalist system and, upon its overthrow, replace it with something new.

Because of its numerical strength and solidarity, the world proletariat is now organizationally stronger than the bourgeoisie of the world, and is far better prepared to turn imperialist wars into class wars.

It cannot be denied that the current attitude of the world proletariat in facing the possibility of world war is different now than in 1914. At the end of the day, the Social Democrats, who in the past delivered up workers to the bourgeois class as canon fodder, are no longer capable of deceiving and betraying the working class. Even in a time before an outbreak of world war, a closely organized communist party has been developed, while the Third International currently hosts an international section in almost every country in the world. At present, the working class of Western Europe under the leadership of the International Union of Workers, Amsterdam (Social Democratic stream), is still holding discussions with the International Union of Workers in Moscow. From this meeting will emerge a union of the two Internationals in the form of one world body, hitherto unseen in the world. If the union takes shape, then the collapse of world capitalism will be even more certain than already.

Just when world capitalism will collapse, cannot be predicted and neither is this prediction necessary. Communists prepare themselves for struggle and activate this struggle, not because they believe in communism as a mysterious world, but because, in line with Marx' dialectical materialism, class struggle must result in the advancement of a very primitive socioeconomic level to an advanced capitalist level and to an even higher level, that is communism.

We communists are never overly eager to ponder problems as to the probability of peace. Sentiments of, respectively, pessimism or optimism could easily take us towards opportunism.

It is an obligation for us to shape the direction of the Communist Party (Party of the Working People), to strengthen it, to take the suffering masses under our leadership, and, finally, to strengthen international bonds and loyalties. If, when the time to act arrives then each communist and each Third International section, at both the national and internal level, must know how to perform its respective task.

CHAPTER 2

THE SITUATION IN INDONESIA

If we describe capitalism as one structure and the countries of the world as piles supporting the edifice, then Indonesia appears as only one of these props. We already know that sooner or later the structure will eventually collapse. However, only practice can determine the shape and extent of the collapse and the way it collapses. It is very possible that all props will immediately fall and, along with it, the whole edifice. However, it is also possible that the props will not fall immediately, but in succession. Each time a prop falls part of the building changes. The economic and political wave which swamped the whole world at the end of the world war almost toppled the weakened world capitalist edifice. Mouldering Russian capitalism was one such pole which could no longer support itself and, as a consequence, gave way. This realignment almost caused the collapse of the whole edifice. However, when a nervous world bourgeoisie was confronted by a rampant world proletariat ready to deliver a death blow, a hand-maiden arrived in the form of the Social Democrats ready to prevent the fall of the edifice of capitalism with the support of the working class and to give an opportunity to the bourgeoisie to repair the building if possible. The collapse of capitalism in Russia was not followed in other capitalist countries. However, the repair work undertaken by the Social Democrats will not be able to prevent the eventual collapse of the whole rotten edifice.

We Indonesian communists cannot hang our political hopes on the prior collapse of the capitalist countries of the world. If colonial capitalism in Indonesia collapses tomorrow or the day after, we must be capable of creating a new, stronger, and more disciplined Indonesia.

Dutch colonial capitalism is supported by the Social Democrats and American capitalism is supported by the Social Democrats. In colonial lands like Egypt, British India, and the Philippines an unstable imperialism is supported by the national bourgeoisie. However, in Indonesia, Dutch imperialism remains vulnerable without hope of support.

The contradictions between the Indonesian

people and Dutch imperialism sharpens with time. The suffering of the masses deepens. The hopes and desires for independence increases with the people's suffering. As time goes on more and more of the Indonesian people are swept up with revolutionary politics. The sharpening conflict between the governing and the governed causes the former to become more brutal and to exercise oppressive measures.

The sweet talking ethical voice has now been changed for a rubber stick and *gemerintjing* sword, in Bandung, Sumedang, Tjiamis and Sidomuljo, Dutch imperialism has already surpassed the limits of the Ethical policy. [11] The implementation of the policy of bludgeons and guns has been officialized by the blood and soul of the proletariat. The Indonesian people are under threat and torture beyond the bounds of humanity and are striving after their birthrights, rights long since recognized in Europe and America, but which Dutch imperialism answers with uncivilized measures. It is clear that rubber sticks and pistols are not capable of making an advancing people retreat.

The mask of reaction has already slipped. The Indonesian people are now already convinced that they cannot hope for anything from the imperialist government. We know, however, that the reactionary class welcomes the repressive actions of Governor General Fok and that the authorities return to study, discuss, and as the question: "Why is the public attitude now different compared to several years ago?" "What policies must we now implement?"

For more than 300 years Dutch imperialism exercised a threatening policy of repression. Never before had politics like this been received with coolness and awareness by the Indonesian people such as occurred on 1 February of this year. Rebellions have occurred in all parts of Indonesia for 300 years and have taken thousands of Indonesian lives, the rebellions of Diponegoro, [12] Aceh, [13] Toli Toli, [14] and others cannot be compared with what happened in Periangan and Madiun. [15] Not because of oaths, talismans, magic voices, or dark symptoms of feudalism which for a long time became a crutch for peoples lives, did the people of Periangan rebel, but because of clear rights and consciousness as human beings, they were encouraged to sacrifice their souls to obtain their rights. So we are not surprised at this time if the authorities say to themselves: "Indonesian people cannot any longer be threatened and repressed". We can only add farewell to the souls of children and... for ever".

Already the power holders are discussing the method to eliminate the sharpening conflict with the Indonesian people. Because more than ever before, the cry of Multatuli[16] will be heard to reverberate in their ears: "If all the people of Java spit on the ground then the Dutch will drown". Ways will also be discussed to improve the economic situation of the people. Similarly, the possibility of giving more political rights to certain Indonesian groups will also be discussed. However, knowing the socio-economic structure of Indonesia, we communists can state emphatically that the holders of authority cannot step outside their narrow bureaucratic environment.

Because, how can Dutch imperialism ameliorate the wrongs already blithely perpetrated down through the centuries? In British India, for example, whenever for many years there has been strong national industry, for the first time a bridge can be created between British capital with national capital, later linking the gaping divide between imperialism and national politics. But from the beginning Dutch imperialism has crushed small industry and national trade, especially in Java. In so doing Chinese capital emerged as an instrument to separate the Indonesian people from Dutch people. All industry in the hands of the Javanese people was killed off soon after Dutch imperialism was established in the East Indies. With the death of industry, so died the Javanese spirit, initiative, and ability, necessary for building a modern national industry based on competition and private property. Dutch imperialism did not seek to obtain any economic compromise with the Indonesian people. Political compromises on the part of the Dutch were just as abstract. Connected with that, each compromise in politics would appear as abstract, something not clear. Increasing the number of members of the Volksraad with two or three more Indonesian members, or giving more political concessions to the Indonesian people, is like one more drop of water on hot steel. It is clear, then, that the Indonesian crisis is not only a political crisis as in Egypt, British India, and in the Philippines, but especially is also an economic crisis, an economic crisis from which Indonesia will not recover for many years.

Nevertheless, while it is clear that Dr. Morgan wishes to pay homage to Dutch imperialism by giving them money loans, the question remains as to whether he is capable of raising himself from his sleeping place. Indonesia is not Austria, Poland, or Germany, where Morgan has shown admirable resourcefulness. The above-mentioned European countries only need capital. Otherwise, the factories, machines, skilled, and unskilled workers are sufficient. In Indonesia, by contrast, which has a literate population of only 5 to 6 percent, which for hundreds of years, has been oppressed and exploited, and with the social importance of the population totally ignored, it would certainly not be possible to raise the technical power even in the space of several years otherwise required to create new industry (metal and textile) capable of successfully entering into competition with Western trade goods. Because of this, Morgan will only lend such money to Dutch imperialism.

It is already clear that America would like to

sow capital in Indonesia, but only in operations which can quickly obtain successful results to the fullest degree, like in oil and rubber. Nowadays, however, we find overproduction of rubber, and, accordingly, America already controls sufficient rubber in Indonesia, so it is unthinkable that it would open more rubber estates. Concerning rubber, we recall that Colyin [17] already transferred all oil tanks in Jambi to British and Dutch oil companies, that is as a colonial monopoly.

For all these reasons, Dutch imperialism will not offer the Indonesian people political and economic concessions, but, will execute the old fashioned uncivilized policy, a legacy of the Dutch East Indies Company (Ost Indische Compangnie). In this logic, the army and navy must be strengthened. These are the kind of responses made to the ever-suffering Indonesian people albeit sufficiently enraged to fully defend their rights.

Marx stated: *"The proletariat have nothing to lose but their chains". This sentence is even more applicable to the Indonesian case. Here non-proletarian demands live in suffering as with industrial workers, because here there is no national industry or national trade. In the likely clash between Dutch imperialism and the Indonesian people there is not one Indonesian who will lose property. In Indonesia we can declaim to all the people. "You have nothing to lose but your chains".*

CHAPTER 3

OBJECTIVES OF THE PKI

The objective of the communist parties of the world is to change the system of capitalism to communism. Until the demise of capitalism and, along with it, the bourgeoisie, communism cannot emerge. Between capitalism and communism is a transitional period. In this interim period the proletariat will exercise dictatorship over the bourgeoisie. This means that the world proletariat will exercise domination over the world bourgeoisie otherwise seeking to reclaim its lost political and economic power and domination. Oppression by the bourgeoisie of the capitalist countries, however, has been changed with the advent of Soviets. The purpose of the Soviets is to eliminate capitalism and to prepare the growth of communism.

Soviet countries have not actually attained communism. To attain communism is a journey of scores of years. The commencement of pure communism means the end of the Soviet state. The Soviet state will end as a state, that is as an instrument of oppression of the proletariat, if the bourgeoisie as oppressor is already eliminated or transformed to become worker members of a communist society.

Under the authority of proletarian dictatorship, big industry, or at least concentrated industry, will be nationalized. This means that this industry will be transferred to proletarian countries. With the nationalization of big industry, personal property will no longer exist but will be transformed into communal property. And thus, anarchy in production will be eliminated, that is to say, the production of daily necessities of no use value, such as occurs in capitalist society. According to the new rationalization, production of goods will be according to social needs. With the elimination of private property and anarchy in production, oppression will also be eliminated. Related to this is the elimination of class distinctions, namely between the proletarian and bourgeois classes.

With the elimination of conflict, the politics of imperialism will no longer obtain, that is to say, capitalist countries using bank capital to assert control over such countries destined as markets for surplus factory production and, consequently, using these countries to obtain raw materials for industry as seed for more capital.

If imperialism no longer remains, so imperialist wars will be eliminated. In a word, communist society will eliminate the creation of private property, anarchy in production, conflict, class, imperialism, and imperialistic war. Instead, communal property, production planning, voluntary production and internationalization, will come into being, while peace, international cooperation, and fraternity, will unite the races of the world.

What is analysed above is the theory of communism which, however, will become a reality if world capitalism simultaneously collapses as almost happened in the first years after the Bolshevik revolution in Russia. It was the Soviet Union that, from the outset of the revolution, quickly formed the basis of pure revolution. Unquestionably, however, it was the Social Democrat betrayal which has, until now, prevented the general collapse of capitalism and forced the Bolsheviks to create steps to retreat in 1921? Steps towards retreating must be understood in the context of economy and tactics. In the economic context, the Soviet state has legalized the return of personal property to the peasantry otherwise comprising 80 percent of the Russian population, and, to the small bourgeoisie in the towns and, along with that, has allowed trade in goods produced on the basis of capitalism. Clearly, these steps are necessary because small factories do not yet have sufficient technical and administrative centralization and also, in this initial stage, because of the growth of an excessively large nationalized bureaucracy. Because private property and trade among peasants and small enterprises is currently allowed, and, given coordination between bureaucracy and economy, Russia can proceed more smoothly. In the final analysis, this shows the wisdom of this policy especially as peasants can be attracted to support the *Negara Buruh* or Worker's State.

The New Economic Policy, as it is so-called, will not only be limited to backward Russia. It also applies in purely capitalist countries such as Germany, England, and America, where around 75 percent of the population are working class, and where the creation of private property and trade by the small bourgeoisie and rural class becomes a certainty. Especially in Indonesia, the New Economic Policy carries very great meaning. Indonesian capitalism is colonial capitalism and does not grow in a regulated way from Indonesian society itself as with capitalism in Europe. Rather, it is forcefully implanted by a Western imperialist country into an Eastern feudal country for the benefit of Western countries.

Indonesian capitalism is still in the initial stage of development, big industry like the machine industry, locomotives, and shipbuilding, and even industry to satisfy the needs of the people like textiles has still not been created. Related to this is the fact that the Indonesian proletariat would endanger the economic life of Indonesia, all the more if the world revolution does not occur. As a consequence, the larger part of the population, that is the non-proletariat, would easily enter into opposition against the small sized Indonesian working class.

To guarantee the economic livelihood of Indonesia in the eventuality of national independence, the non-proletarian population must be given an opportunity (within a limited scale) to initiate private property with capitalist enterprise. More than that, the country must give then both material, as well as moral assistance, to increase their production. Undoubtedly big industry will have to be quickly nationalized. *Only then can the economic activities of the people be developed without raising the future anxiety of other classes or groups. Only then can an economic balance between the proletariat and non-proletariat be achieved and strengthened.*

Whenever a balance economy is achieved, then a political balance will automatically follow suit. Necessarily, the Indonesian working class cannot advance very far in either the economic or political arenas. *Even if the working class achieve the most in the coming national independence struggle neither can they neglect the non-proletarian elements.* This is even more the case if the non-proletarian elements in the struggle obtain stakes as large or larger so that even an interim pure Soviet system in Indonesia cannot yet be planned. Of course we must always remember that the quality and quantity of the working class is low, while non-proletarian elements, even larger in size, are objectively revolutionary, with the exception of all those classified as small land owners. Because in Free Indonesia, the non-proletariat people must be given an opportunity to express their voices. However, if in the likely forthcoming national independence war, the working class creates a pioneer force from all the people, then big industry will fall into its hands along with political power. The political balance with non-proletarian elements will easily be obtained wherever it is most important for Free Indonesia.

Whenever the national and economic balance is obtained, then it follows that Indonesia will develop in the economic and political field. The speed towards the direction of a pure Soviet, and following that, to communism, depends on the international situation and more so on the development of industry in Indonesia itself.

NATIONAL PROGRAM OF THE PKI

A. ECONOMY

1. To nationalize factories and mines like coal mines, tin, oil, and gold.
2. To nationalize forest resources and modern agricultural works like sugar mills, rubber, tea, coffee, cinchona, coconut, indigo and tapioca.
3. To nationalize communications and transport systems.
4. To nationalize banks, company partnerships and big trading companies.
5. To electrify Indonesia by building new industry with the help of the state, such as machine factories, textiles, and slipways for the construction of ships.
6. To create cooperation between people

with the help of cheap credit from the state.

7. To render help to the peasantry with cattle and implements to improve agriculture and to build state experimental agricultural stations.

8. To transfer big population groups at State expense from Java to the outer islands.

9. To divide uncultivated land among unemployed and landless peasants as well as offering financial assistance to work the land.

10. To eliminate the remainder of feudal land and private land and divide it among the poorest peasantry and the proletariat.

B. POLITICS

1. The speedy and unconditional independence of Indonesia.

2. The creation of the Federal Republic from the various islands of Indonesia.

3. The speedy convocation of a national meeting represented by all peoples and religions in Indonesia.

4. The quick conferral of full political rights on the Indonesian people, both men and women.

C. SOCIAL

1. A minimum wage, a seven hour working

day and improvement in working hours and workers' livelihood.

2. Attention to the working environment with the recognition of the workers' right to strike.

3. Division of profits among workers in big industries.

4. Creation of a workers council in big industry.

5. Separation of church and state and recognition of freedom of religion.

6. Granting of social, economic, and political rights to Indonesian nationals both men and women.

7. The nationalization of big homes and the construction of new houses to be allocated to workers in state enterprises.

D. STUDY AND EDUCATION

1. Compulsory for all Indonesian children up to 17 years of age in Indonesian language as the language of communication with English language as the principal foreign language.

2. Elimination of the current system of education and creation of a practical system linked to the present and future needs of Indonesia.

3. Improvement and increase in the number of schools for agriculture and trade experts and improvement and increase in the number of

schools for high officials in the technical and administrative field.

E. MILITARY

1. Elimination of the imperialist army and creation of a people's military to defend the Indonesian Republic.
2. Elimination of military cantonments and all regulations which restrict and regulate such aspects of a soldier's life as place of domicile, while offering them better and higher wages.
3. Granting of full rights to soldiers to create organizations and meetings.

F. POLICE AND JUSTICE

1. The separation of *pangreh-praja* (civil service), Police and Judiciary.
2. Granting full rights to all accused to offering them protection against the courts in the face of justice and freeing the accused in 24 hours if proof and evidence is perfectly clear.
3. Each case which possesses a basis in law must be completed in a period of five days following general procedure.

G. ACTION PLAN

1. Demand a seven hours working day,

minimum wages, and better working conditions and livelihood for workers.

2. Recognition of Workers' Union and the right to strike.

3. Organization and peasant's economic and political rights.

4. Elimination of *poenale sanctie*. [18]

5. The elimination of laws and regulations which oppress political movements, such as governmental power to:
    a. Exile any person considered a danger to the state.
    b. Forbid strikes.
    c. Forbid and dissolve meetings.
    d. Forbid press publication.
    e. Forbid the giving of lessons and the full acknowledgment of independence movements.

6. Demand rights to demonstrate: mass demonstrations throughout Indonesia in opposition to political and economic oppression like taxation, the quick release of political prisoners, and the return of political exiles, mass action must be strengthened with public strikes in opposition to the government.

7. Demand to eliminate the Volksraad, Raad van Indie dan Algemeene Secretaris [19] and create a National Assembly from where will be chosen an implementing body responsible to the National Assembly.

SHORT CLARIFICATION CONCERNING THE PROGRAM

There is still not a single political party in Indonesia which has gone as far as clarifying its program, although the two parties of intellectuals, namely, Budi Utomo and Nasional Indische Partij, as well as the mass-based Sarekat Islam, can at short notice, draw up economic and political demands. They also hold firm to the same word, independence. However, they cannot achieve a concrete analysis of the Indonesian economic and social situation. As a result, they cannot achieve their program. A program cannot be just a "wish list", but must be based on the specific social and economic foundation of the country.

Additionally, the PKI cannot yet organize what it really wants to achieve, either in this present juncture under imperialism, or, in the time when imperialism is crushed. It is already locked into the present. A program can't cover everything. No, there can be no meaningful revolutionary program, without a revolutionary movement. Nevertheless, any revolutionary movement which does not possess a clear theoretical basis and firmly organized revolutionary goal or program will not achieve success and will become a tool for capitalism.

As proof we can take one example; Budi Utomo, National Indische Partij, and Sarekat Islam. Inevitably, in the initial stages the three of them were revolutionary, yet not one of them could organize revolutionary goals. Without question, leadership and discipline caused the ruin of these parties, although the principal reason was failure to clarify their goals (program), and failure to clearly analyse the path to be followed (tactics).

The revolutionary movement in Indonesia always remains. If this movement wants to obtain results – and the time is ripe – then we must organize a national program and give it wide publicity.

We think, that our program is in accordance with the Indonesian economic and social situation. We can, accordingly, step up our demands, without damaging ourselves. In other areas we cannot retreat one step. This program well accords with all possibilities, both international and national, if, sooner or later, world capitalism collapses, and the Indonesian people succeed in obtaining the fullest support from the proletariat of the West, then this program can be used as a strong basis to shape the communist edifice. If, in the near future, we are forced to wage the national struggle on our own, then this program includes sufficient elements to raise up and concentrate the energy of the still slumbering Indonesian people, precisely the energy needed in order to obtain national independence.

Then, after having obtained independence, we can also defend it better. With the energy found in Indonesia in the immediate aftermath of the winning of independence we can quickly make steps towards international communism and with greater hopes.

If we can execute this program in an independent Indonesia, and this independence is clearer than so-called independence in many countries of the modern world, then Indonesian workers will own big industry and will exercise good authority in the economy as well as in the state politics. Exploitation and repression, such as currently suffered by the workers of Japan, America, and England, will no longer remain. The social links between slavery and employer will give way to equality and independence. Profits amounting to millions, now flowing into the pockets of the usurers of Zorgvliet (Den Haag), will be used to advance Indonesian industry (textiles and machine factories, shipyards, and hydroelectricity plants). These profits, in turn, will be used to assist financing peasants, small traders, and small industry as mentioned. In short, our program not only covers workers in the narrow meaning of the word, but almost all of the Indonesian people.

We have the courage to say this, not because we want to promise paradise to all men, but to stress their independence. The importance of independence strongly suggests that non-proletarians among the peasantry, small traders, small industrial workers, and intellectuals must also be given a share of the economy if the workers nationalize big industry. Because national capital is very small, and because of the anxieties created by fear of workers' nationalization, and because more than 90 percent of the population live in suffering and misery, then cooperation between the proletariat and non-proletariat, then slowly will disappear all obstacles to creating big industry on a higher technical level, all for one, and one for all. Small industry must be made aware that state industry can achieve success, faster, better, and cheaper than they can.

Whenever they become aware of this, they will willingly surrender themselves to the State enterprise and will leave their small enterprise.

If this economic process, that is the investment of small industry into large-scale State industry can work in the context of an independent Indonesia, then the politics of the small bourgeoisie will give way to the politics of the international working class.

It is already clear at this juncture, that the non-proletariat in Indonesia, while revolutionary in appearance, are narrow nationalists in their politics. They only seek to wipe out imperialism, not to eliminate poverty. However, the Indonesian working class consider people who are not proletarian as not fighters. For Indonesia there are signs of optimism, in that non-workers submit to the leadership of the workers (formed into the PKI). Cooperation between proletariat and non-proletariat already reveals itself as a living force. In Priangan, where capitalism has not penetrated deeply, and where small bourgeoisie have a certain role, non proletarian elements under the leadership of the communists have shown bravery and resourcefulness. To the PKI falls the task of raising up the albeit sleeping masses in Sumatra, Kalimantan, Sulawesi, and in other places. Gradually, the Sarekat Rakyat must become organized [against] all imperialist enemies. If the population in the big towns of Java and outside of Java are made aware that the PKI program seeks to raise the security of the people in general and does not neglect the importance of the non-proletariat, then they will surrender themselves to PKI leadership.

It is an historical imperative that the PKI must assume the revolutionary leadership. Wherever national capital is lacking, the industrial working class – as the class most closely linked and numerous – is the class capable of organizing the economy and politics strongly and with clear and specific aims. Because the non-proletariat of Indonesia do not constitute a fixed class, it is extremely difficult to form a class orientation, otherwise giving firm leadership to the Indonesian people. This is proven by the failure of non-proletarian parties like Budi Utomo, National Indische Partij, and Sarekat Indij. If the non-proletarian people of Indonesia wish to struggle to achieve independence then they will have to achieve the support of the industrial workers with awareness of political organization and workers' unions capable of crushing the political and economic apparatus of the imperialists.

Also, after national independence is achieved, strong cooperation between proletarian and non-proletariat is an absolute condition. If this cooperation is ruptured, and, if increasingly, non-proletarian elements become enemies of the industrial working class, then national independence will only give new life to national slavery. Not so far distant from Indonesia can be found such agents of international plunder as British, American, and Japanese imperialism poised to launch their imperialist attacks at the first good opportunity. As long as Indonesia is firmly united and in solidarity, they postpone their attempts to seize Indonesia. But as soon as internal dissension sets in they will soon seek to implement a divide and rule policy (splitting the people into groups so as to rule over them). Indonesia consists of many islands existing at various levels of civilization, offering a good field for international plunder. The areas outside Java, otherwise revealing petty bourgeois characteristics, could easily be set up to oppose Java which is very proletarian. A situation such as in China, Mexico, and South America, will be experienced by Indonesians, that is playing one off against each other in a situation of chronic or periodically erupting civil war.

A situation like this has to be guarded against so as not to let it happen! But not with high-flown and empty doctrine. Only a program which is really directed to the struggle for material benefits of the whole people and carried out with justice can create a loyal group otherwise capable of crushing imperialism. But not only that, a group is needed to distance itself for a time before finally pioneering the way to international communism.

The question is whether we have the right to undertake a program like that. We can only reply with several words. For over 300 years Indonesia has been trampled over and exploited endlessly and with thousands of souls sacrificed for Dutch imperialism. Hundreds of millions of guilders have flowed into the pockets of the clippers of Dutch coupons. *And Dutch capital in Indonesia as mentioned in our program* on nationalization only represents one part of what was exploited in Indonesia over 300 years. So we still cannot change the souls of the peasants and workers of Indonesia, whether in Aceh, Java, Jambi, and in such other places which have already protested against the robbery and killing.

The final question is, whether or not we are capable of seizing national independence and defending it. We can reply to this in several words. If we are capable of attracting fifty million of the Indonesian population to our program and if, following this, the PKI and Sarekat Rakyat posses sufficient consciousness, and discipline, then the way of the people's movements which have been oppressed for 300 years will not be neglected.

TACTICS AND STRATEGY

Of course, aside from out program, the success of our revolution actually depends upon our tactics and strategy. The meaning of these two words cannot be separated. We can say that tactics are part of an overall strategy. It is tactics which links to our revolutionary operations in any given place at any given time. But strategy determines our operations for the duration of the revolutionary struggle. To deploy a tactical strike is to use part or all of our strength for a limited objective. A strategic strike, by contrast, is a final action where we mobilize all our strength to win strategic victory, to break the enemy organization and then to crush it.

One example of a tactical action was the VSTP strike in 1923 and the protest meetings in Priangan.[20] Even so, we witnessed little evidence of consciousness in this event. A pure tactical strike must be exercised with greater awareness and better preparation. Additionally, it should not be viewed as a strike which stands on its own but as a preparation or as a part of a strategic strike. *A tactical strike in Indonesia must serve as a prelude to a strategic strike.*

A decisive strategic strike can guarantee greater hope if, in launching a tactical strike, we display bravery, skill and perseverance. But this does not necessarily mean that we should fight to the end. Rather, we must know when to take a step backward, when to fight hard, and how to achieve victory wherever one of our sections is knocked out. Necessarily, our political organization in the PKI, the Sarekat Rakyat, ad Sarekat Sekerja, must continue to struggle, until the general staff of the PKI can plan the strategic strike. If our political and economic organizations can demonstrate enough skill, discipline, consciousness, will, and motivation, then, at a later juncture, every tactical struggle can be turned into a strategic struggle.

If we can commence to launch a strategic struggle it won't only depend on the quality of our organization but our economic and political situation, both inside and outside the country. However, the strategic strike will stand a better chance of success if every economic and political action of ours is launched with success. This means that if we fail to obtain full success then we can at least prevent a defeat that may well weaken the organization over a long period of time (but not preventing the struggle...). Of course, the political or economic struggle in a capitalist society is relative. Moreover, if even one of our organizations is defeated, rendering it out of action over a long period of time, then automatically, the time to launch a strategic blow will be delayed. On the other hand, if even one of our organizations achieves a tactical victory, then not only will the victorious organization win advantage, but so will the revolutionary movements in Indonesia. Then, belief in leadership, confidence in final victory, and will to struggle will increase.

Such a war strategy is not the same as a revolutionary strategy. In a war situation both the quality and the quantity of forces is constant although this changes somewhat in the case of revolutionary forces. In the latter case, both the size and kind of forces undergo a high tide and an ebbing. This rise and fall is governed by the economic and political situation of the country. If all the population lives in a situation of extreme suffering, such as the case in Indonesia at the moment, if the measures taken are cruel and exercised narrowly, then the wave of revolutionary spirit will rise up all over the country so that the General Staff of the revolution will spontaneously attract forces of a size never before experienced. If, for example, the PKI at the present can rally 50,000 members, then as soon as the Inlansche Verpendin [21] or other economic pressures begin to bite, then the entire people will take shelter behind the communist flag, especially if we know how to assiduously sow propaganda and vigorously defend our program and position.

Because revolutionary forces are subject to more of a fluctuation than conventional forces, then the general staff of a revolutionary force must have far more planning and foresight than the general command of a conventional force.

From the outset, revolutionary forces have to calculate their physical strength as well as that of their opponents in any future contingency. Besides, tactics have to be fine-tuned along with the fluctuating situation and must, accordingly, be sufficiently flexible. Revolutionary forces also have to take much more into account the moral situation than the case of the general staff of a conventional force in a conventional war as this is an important matter indeed for a revolutionary force.

Even if a conventional war is in many ways different from a revolutionary struggle there are still many points of similarity as well as points of difference. The following laws that hold in the case of a strategic war also hold for a revolutionary strategy:

1. The level of offensive and initiative.
2. Concentrating strength in an advantageous place and time.

THE LEVEL OF OFFENSIVE AND INITIATIVE

In every kind of struggle, initiative is an important principle. Those who take prior initiative have certain advantage which cannot be resumed by their opponents. Because they are the first to initiate action they can create a new situation for their opponents. Because of it, their opponents cannot think of a new plan by themselves, however tied they are to the situation just created. In this way their plan awaits to be crushed by those who take the initiative. Besides this, in overcoming wishes and actions, the passive is obliged to await the attack of those who take the initiative.

If we in the revolutionary struggle do not first seize the initiative, then our opponents will gain advantage in winning over our desires and actions so that we are forced into a crippling passive situation. If, for example, the enemy sought to crush one among others of the Sarekat Sekerja or our national groups and it already took prior initiative then we would feel pressured and uncertainty because we would not know how and when it will act. However, if we seek to avert this situation by taking prior initiatives then we will also obtain, besides moral advantage, the edge in overcoming our opponent's schemes already under way, possibly also being able to crush them.

The end of the struggle that takes initiative is offensive. Those who attack first have initiative and overcome the plans and conduct of their opponents. But the shape of a good offensive is an offensive that is carried out defensively. Even if our aim is no less than the elimination of imperialism and capitalism, we are forced by the situation to launch an attack in a defensive form. We prepare our attack after being threatened and attacked. Against the actions of our reactionary opponents, we base agitation, protest, or action which brings us closer to our final aims.

Of the final determining blow, we can only obtain victory if we also take defensive initiative so that the final determining blow can shape our aims. Beginning from now, the Sarekat Sekerja and our other political organizations, must possess offensive spirit.

CONCENTRATING STRENGTH IN AN ADVANTAGEOUS PLACE AND TIME

The aim of every offensive is to attack and overwhelm the defences of the enemy with large forces with the intention to break its organizational link and to finally crush it for ever.

Our main struggle organization, the Sarekat Sekerja Politik, should, if the time is ripe, be rapidly deployed to a place where we can inflict upon the enemy the greatest disaster, namely where they concentrate their main forces.

If we consider Indonesia as our battlefield, then we will find that the military, political, and economic strength of the Dutch imperialists is not centred in one place, but dispersed. Military strength is centred in Priangan. The political centre now in Batavia may later may be shifted to Priangan. However, both Batavia and Priangan really do not have an economic base. We only find this situation in the Bengawan-Solo or Surakarta valley, [22] that is to say, in the residencies of Yogjakarta, Solo, Madiun, Kediri, and Surabaya, where industry, including factories, transport companies, banks, and other concerns, are concentrated.

Where else can a revolutionary offensive already in advance preparation obtain such great success?

If military, political, and economic strength is centred in one town, as often happens in Europe, then it becomes our obligation to enter the town beforehand to plan our revolutionary organization in advance of launching a first revolutionary offensive. If our plans prove successful there, then other parts of Indonesia would – more or less – automatically fall into our hands.

However, because Dutch imperialist power is dispersed over several centres, we too must accordingly divide our revolutionary forces and select the place that is most important for our victory.

If we consider the matter carefully, then we arrive at the conclusion that the most advantageous place for us to storm would be the Bengawan-Solo valley. Clearly, we have a greater hope of seizing economic and political power and defence in this locale than in Batavia and Priangan. In the Bengawan-Solo valley are concentrated industrial workers and poverty-stricken peasants, who will contribute the energy, not only for the seizure, but also as a technical and economic condition to defend this seizure. In Batavia or Priangan political or military victory would be difficult to obtain and defend compared to the Bengawan-Solo valley because of the lack of technical and economic conditions necessary to defend the seizure. Political or military victory in Batavia or Priangan would be more difficult to defend than in the Bengawan_Solo valley, because of the lack of technical or economic factors [as mentioned]. A modern political and military victory could only be defended if we possess the basic conditions of economic power, factories, industries, transport corporations, and banking institutions.

From what has been mentioned above we can draw the conclusion that we must mobilize our main forces to the Bengawan-Solo valley so that our revolutionary offensive can confirm our overall strategy. If we can maintain our position temporarily in the Bengawan-Solo valley, and also make an attack on other centres of economic power such as the east coast of Sumatra, Palembang, and east Kalimantan, and also in such centres of economic and military power, as Batavia, Bandung, Magelang, Malang, and Aceh, then we can attack or successfully defend the

Bengawan-Solo valley as the basis for an Indonesian Republic. Increasingly, if our voice and influence can sway the Army and Navy forces, then Dutch imperialism cannot easily deploy its military power. The enthusiastic voices of workers from the Bengawan-Solo valley will surely be heard by the workers of Asia, Europe, and America and foreign imperialism will not easily attack and kill the Indonesian workers. Besides, the Third International will work to call to a halt the killing by the imperialists.

Although the Bengawan-Solo valley is ideal for our victory, places like Priangan, and especially Aceh, and Ternate, are vital for the creation of diversions designed to mislead the enemy. When we have made a successful attack on these places the enemy will be forced to divide its strength otherwise concentrated in Java and obliged to send part of it to the remote areas. For the revolutionary movement matters like this are inevitably important for morale. Besides, if Dutch imperialism continues to repress revolutionary resistance with force so then will the cost increase for the imperialists. Consequently, it will be forced to raise even higher taxes from the suffering peoples. This will only further stimulate dissatisfaction and raise the level of revolutionary consciousness.

A victory in Priangan, Aceh, and Ternate, seen from the tactical perspective, is very important and can lead the way to strategic victory. The strategic victory that we will then launch in the Bengawan-Solo valley will appear as a sword of Damocles hanging over the head of Dutch imperialism.

Connected with the importance of the Bengawan-Solo valley for Indonesian independence is our revolutionary duty to give more prominence to economic centres than hitherto. It is our revolutionary duty to organize and coordinate the mass industrial proletariat and peasant class and to train them for continuing action to seize economic and political power.

LEVEL OF CONSCIOUSNESS, WILL AND DISCIPLINE

In every movement consciousness plays an important role. By revolutionary consciousness we take our lead from Marx's dialectical materialism. Following Marx, we can determine that currently almost all the Indonesian people possess revolutionary spirit. But there is a big difference between the revolutionary state of industrial workers and the state of small owners like peasants, traders, and small producers. Subjectively, the former is revolutionary when they not only seek to eliminate political power but also economic power by means of the elimination of private property and a capitalist system of production. But subjectively, the small property holders are not revolutionary because they do not wish to eliminate private property and capitalist production. On the other hand, they seek more property themselves. However, vis-à-vis imperialism, they have a revolutionary attitude. They seek the creation of a national government and national independence. Because of that, their objectives are revolutionary.

In matters of organization, tactics, and strategy we cannot involve both industrial workers and non-proletarian elements. Such a conflation will not bring strength but only simply and solely bring weakness. Even if the above elements both struggle to oppose imperialism, their basis and aims for struggle remain different. Such differences notwithstanding, people cannot forget the necessity of working together because both non-proletarian goals and the ultimate goals of the industrial proletariat will only be exercised after the crushing of imperialism. The tactics of the PKI against non-proletarian elements is to raise up their material importance so that they are flexible. They must be capable of raising up revolutionary energy and potential within the non-proletarian elements. They must also be able to coordinate their force with proletarian force. If it succeeds, then Indonesian independence can said to be confirmed.

Revolutionary consciousness must be matched by revolutionary will. Consciousness alone is not sufficient. Clearly, the Indonesian people, enslaved for 300 years, cannot prevail in a single day against one imperialism undoubtedly assisted by other imperialisms. There is no question that in some places the PKI will experience setbacks. It is also possible that in some places the PKI will be forced to prosecute more underground actions. However, in all these circumstances, it cannot and must not lose its courage and ideological direction. On the other hand, we are convinced that it will be more active, more experienced, and more brave. The PKI understands that the downfall of Dutch imperialism and the revolutionary power of the Indonesian people does not simply rest on the Djojo Bojo myth [23] or other peddlers of *djamu* (nostrums), but, rather, its beliefs are grounded upon a firm social economic analysis of Indonesian society. The conflict that ruptures the peace between the governing body and the governed in Indonesia will strengthen the struggle.

Consciousness and will can be exercised locally if the PKI possesses discipline. All members, sections, and organizations of the PKI must carry out decisions of the centre, honestly, and actively. One section must rally to help another section in adversity. It must advance if the leadership views it necessary, and retreat backwards if the struggle orders it to do so. A struggle can only obtain success if the General Staff can have full confidence in all the army.

STRATEGIC BLOW

The final strategic blow will succeed if the following conditions are fulfilled:

1. The party possesses iron discipline.
2. The Indonesian people remain under the leadership of the PKI
3. Enemies both inside and outside the country are divided.

If the first condition is not fulfilled, we cannot uphold secrecy. It is often the case that a responsible member follows his own opinions without waiting for the central decision making. Or, he exercises his opinion while still knowing that it conflicts with the central opinion. An undisciplined attitude or character in a true revolutionary struggle not only endangers the concerned leadership and section but also the whole movement.

Revolutionary discipline has a similarity with military discipline at this point: namely that decisions have to be taken. However, one is different from the other in this matter: namely that revolutionary discipline is not only a desire to surrender (sebelum dauh). While a military General Staff does not expect its soldiers to understand orders which are given, in the case of a Revolutionary General Staff, the first conditions are that members must really understand decisions that have to be undertaken. This just doesn't mean only decisions but that all members must also understand absolute obedience in the implementation of decisions, even if the decision conflicts with their own opinion.

Each revolutionary decision can only be taken with precision after considerable discussion. In each discussion every member possesses full rights to advance and defend his opinions and oppose or support the opinions of other people. After the final voting he has the right to defend his opinions as strongly as possible, so that he can exercise all spiritual influence over the Party's decisions. But if the majority make a decision conflicting with his own, and he does not agree with it, then he must bow to that decision and, as a member or leader, he must carry it out with obedience and dispatch. If this does not happen, it is not possible for the revolutionary strength of the Party to act outside as a harmonized mass. A Party where each member holds strong to his own opinion and sabotages the decision of the Party cannot be tolerated.

Thus the second condition is not yet fulfilled. It is very clear that the PKI is currently one among other parties that can be said to be a party of the Indonesian people. Budi Utomo, Pasundan, Perserikatan Minahasa [24] and other small parties can, with difficulty, defend themselves within narrow boundaries. But a party can only become a national party beyond narrow boundaries, if it exerts great strength.

Currently, only the PKI is capable of operating in any place throughout the islands. Yet, it cannot be said that it has organized all layers of people and taken them under its leadership. It is still not enough even if all the oppressed Indonesian people hold out sympathy to the PKI. Nevertheless, when the time comes, millions of the oppressed will follow the call of the PKI. Not only in victory but also in defeat, loyalty and obedience to the PKI as the people's revolutionary party must be fixed and unchangeable.

We must recognize that our propaganda and agitation in areas outside Java and also inside Java itself is still not concrete and strong enough and, because of it, not sufficiently penetrated. An insufficiency of strength and tools an insufficiency of knowledge concerning the regional situation outside Java is the main reason our revolutionary power is still concentrated in

Java and our activities are still limited to Java. Even if, here and there, communist power has already blossomed (Ternate, Aceh, and in other places) the majority in areas outside Java appear to us as country bumpkins or adolescents (Jambi and Palembang), self-satisfied, child-minded, in the dark, and still not grouped with the rest of Indonesia. Big mining operations, such as gold mining, tin, oil, coal, and agriculture like tea, and rubber, still have not experienced change. Bandjarmasin and Aceh, where fanatical wars are waged under the banner of Islam are still foreign to us. In the above-mentioned areas we still have not won influence among the peasantry. Not only have we run into reaction there, but we have scarcely penetrated the difficulties of living of these nationals and their way of thinking.

If we, in areas outside Java – also in Java as well – wish to raise up the levels of energy to the level of the revolutionary movement, then propaganda and agitation must be harmonized with the local situation with all its differences throughout Indonesia, more so than we have already achieved. We have to influence the people of Jambi, Banjar, and Aceh, who are more or less under the sway of religion. If we still cannot join up with them then we cannot speak of revolutionary leadership. It follows that we must then show that our program seeks to uplift material life. We have to be capable to clarify that all obstacles experienced by small traders, peasants, and small producers, in areas outside Java at this time will disappear after the elimination of imperialism. If non-proletarian elements, mostly outside Java, become aware that in national independence, they, and not only industrial workers, will profitably produce material goods, then they will join with the proletariat in the struggle to oppose imperialism. If Rome could not be built in a day, then educating and organizing 50 million people even though oppressed for hundreds of years will need time. Nevertheless, precisely because of the ever rising oppression and reaction, the PKI will be nicely assisted.

Even if in short time the party can be disciplined and the larger part of the population placed under our leadership, we must still know beforehand the situation in the enemy camp, both among those in the country and outside, before we can launch a decisive strike. The more shattered the situation of our opponents, the more advantage for us. We can say that the opposition by Dutch imperialism in the country succeeds in confronting the Indonesian people. The case is not the same as in Europe. The bourgeoisie, formed into the Conservative Party, the Liberal Party, and other radical parties, in confronting revolutionary workers, appear to be unified, but in fact deep divisions appeared among them. The Social Democrats vacillate between the bourgeoisie and the Democrats. The division between the European bourgeoisie in

Indonesia, especially as they spring from a different race than the local working class, are not large in number, so the Indonesian people can obtain more meaningful benefits in their division. No matter the temporary solidarity of the Dutch bourgeoisie in the face of the Indonesian people, the unity of 100,000 is nothing alongside the solidarity of 50,000,000.

However, enemies outside the country (imperialism) British, American, and Japanese, confront Indonesia in a disunited fashion. Between American and Japanese imperialism there are no elements of unity and solidarity. Sooner or later, these two imperialisms must defend their power in the Pacific ocean with arms. *Still no one can predict with certainty the outbreak of war between Japan and America.*

The economic and political conflict between Japan and America constraining the peace in East Asia has already repeatedly occurred and requires no analysis here. It certainly can be affirmed that Britain will stand with America so that the Japanese armada will, compared with the American fleet, be at a ratio of 3:10. One question of importance is, which of the three mentioned imperialist powers will examine the current international situation and bring on the new world war?

Of course there is one certainty, that America will prosecute its policy of Pacific Penetration wherever it achieves victory in economic competition. A new world war is not essential for the United States to extend the area of influence, but this problem will bring danger, namely, that the international working class under the leadership of Moscow will transform world war into class war.

In the Kingdom of Japan itself there are those who oppose the imminent Japan-America war. The natural disaster caused by an earthquake in 1923 caused great damage to the Japanese economy at least as can be seen from the outside. [25] That disaster for Japan means that it will require great effort and long time before it can economically recover to a level prior to the disaster. The movement to democratize Japan from an autocracy led by the middle class and assisted by the entire working class continues. This movement is strengthened because unemployment in the country increases (according to the latest news more than three million) including many victims from the middle classes. By appearances, the movement to democratize takes a dangerous form, so that the militarist clique that holds authority over the entire political and military apparatus in Japan is obliged to give many political concessions. According to news from early this year the parliamentary system in Japan is modernizing and creating voting rights so that the number of voters will increase from three to twelve million. In creating it, the militarist clique does not wish to create a new war (in this matter the militarist clique can defend the autocracy against the liberal middle classes). Late last year Japan already reached an agreement with the Soviet Union. Even if this agreement is directed against the Anglo-American alliance, it is also used to win the blind loyalty of the working class and middle class who hate and fear the onset of a new war on the basis of the slogan that Japan "seeks peace with whomever". The above-mentioned economic and political pacts show that internally Japan still does not possess power and unity that is desired to dare to oppose itself against world authority like America and England at this time.

It never easy to obtain independence right off. During the last war we know that not one of the colonized countries (French Indochina, British India, and Egypt) wished to sacrifice their struggle for independence. For Indonesia likewise, it also cannot be asserted that even in the eventuality of a Pacific war we can obtain a good opportunity to claim independence. Precisely the matter depends upon the problem, who will win, and how long the war will endure? But it is clear that in the meantime in the seas surrounding Indonesia the British, American, and Dutch naval armada is being prepared. For Indonesia, it is still not an easy problem to speak about independence, much less to seize independence. Anglo-America seeks absolute tranquility and security in Indonesia and will consider any disturbance as an enemy of peace.

More than that because the British seek to defend the link between Singapore and British Australia they will take advantage of the first opportunity to occupy Indonesia if Dutch imperialism is thrown out.

Similar difficulties will be confronted by Indonesia if after more than ten years the Singapore Naval base [26] and the Dutch naval defences will have been completed. The connection between Singapore and Australia will become clearer and the defence of Indonesia by Anglo-American imperialism will be entrusted to the Dutch fleet.

It is apparent that intra-imperialist conflict is beneficial to us. However the problem is this: should we have to await the outbreak of war or should we now claim national independence and use all our devices to obtain it now?

Because we know in advance that an impending Pacific War may still not bring independence, and because we cannot wait while the Dutch fleet and the Singapore Navy base are set up as an encircling force, now is likely to be the right opportunity for Indonesia to demand national independence. This opinion is also strengthened on the following basis:

1. We cannot make our revolutionary tactics entirely dependent upon the outbreak of a Japan-America war. Tactics like that would be opportunist and dangerous. There is no people that can endure long in a tense situation with

imminent threats. Increasingly, if in two or three years the threats still do not become a reality, then psychological tension will automatically become widespread. Revolutionary tension will become a way of life if it is based on material conditions actually experienced by the people. Only **if** our revolutionary agitation is based on clear suffering experienced by the people under the authority of Dutch at this point in time, will we be capable of convincing the masses of our propaganda, so that the dissatisfaction of the masses will change to become a mass desire and mass actions. Following on from this we now strive to advance our goals and be prepared to face the consequences of our revolutionary agitation.

2. There is a possibility that the Japan-America war will not transpire and that a *periode pasifistis* or period of peace must precede the social revolution throughout the world. If we make our actions dependent upon world war and the world revolution then there is a possibility that we will lose our leadership role over the Indonesian people. Because of it our Party will remain mired in dogma while the masses will take their own path. This path would lead to the outbreak of local rebellions or individual or anarchistic actions (*anarsistis*). Of course in their dissatisfaction Indonesian people will follow our revolutionary leadership as long as possible at least while the leadership manifests itself as an out-growth of this

revolutionary direction.

3. We have not yet reflected as to whether immediate Indonesian independence would endanger peace in the Pacific. Such independence could cause an outbreak of the Pacific War. However, it cannot be said that the world powers out of fear of social revolution will delay the outbreak of war for long. In fact, this would advantage rather than disadvantage the possibility of Indonesian independence. Last year we saw in China that there was not a single large imperialist power that dared to carve up China and occupy it even though they had the opportunity to do this. Precisely at this time in China, civil war flared up such that big foreign capital interests in China suffered bankruptcy. Only the fear of intra-imperialist war caused them to stay their distance. Every player seeks to occupy the best part of China and, accordingly, runs into conflict with its enemy in making its pitch. Because each imperialist seeks to occupy prime position in China, the result is that none takes anything.

Viewed from the perspective of trade and strategy the situation of Indonesia in the Pacific is very important, indeed, such that there no imperialist power would allow it to be occupied by any other strong country. Every endeavour to divide up Indonesia by the imperialist powers would quickly lead to disagreement and war. Even more so, if Indonesia itself does not just remain passive but exploits the division of its enemies.

If Indonesia presently becomes a colony of Anglo-America then the hopes of Japan to spread its influence to South and West Asia will permanently fail. The Japanese aspirations for an "Asia for the Asians", that is Asia under the heel of Japan will be futile. Japan, already forbidden access to America and Australia, will be permanently isolated in East Asia.

Moreover, Anglo-America will not permit Japan to occupy any point in Indonesia. Yeseboru Takakoshi, [27] long-time mouth-piece (*terompet?*) of the Japanese militarists, wages a major war, and shook the imperialist world when he showed just how important were the Sunda and Malacca Straits. However, these two Straits, each of them strategic points in Indonesia, if occupied by Japan, would mean a pistol in the chest of the British government.

If we conclude as to the situation of the enemy, both inside and outside the country, then we can say: "Fortress Holland in an economic and political sense". It remains in a clear adversary situation apropos the revolutionary people. If, besides this, they don't win, then they will strike tomorrow. Foreign imperialists remain in a troubled and divided condition and **in** the future years it will not be possible for them to meddle in Indonesian affairs without risking world war.

To ask the question, when is the right time to

mount political actions for unlimited and complete independence, we must reply: "Now and not later". If at a later date we are not presented with such a moment, then we must say, "we allowed an opportunity to pass".

Now is the time for the PKI inside the country to struggle to create its own organization, one possessed with sufficient courage and strength to seize and defend national independence. If, presently, after many small and large quarrels here and there, now using political organizations, then using organizations of the Sarekat Sekerja, we can show consciousness, will, wisdom, ambition, then we can finally strike our revolutionary blow, one that will be heard by the other conquered countries of Asia as well as by the shackled workers of Europe.

THE INDONESIAN CONSULTATIVE COUNCIL

In contrast to the pessimism enshrined in the writings of Voltaire, d'Alembert, [28] Rousseau, and others, the French aristocracy preceded by spendthrift kings and even more spendthrift queens led an extremely luxurious life. It appears that there was no other view of life than that contained in the assertions: "After me, the deluge".

The way of life of the nobility and kings and their luxurious expenses on full display to the miserable people as if the world was created for no other purpose, except for them to pay tax. Misery, illness, and hunger, are found everywhere. And because of it the dissatisfaction of the masses increases.

Peasants, workers, and bourgeoisie, under the above-mentioned leadership, will one day join themselves together as one to claim radical political changes. The creation of a "National Consultative Council" representing the whole people speaking for the nation, itself the successful culmination of the determined political struggle, can then be convened. However, the nobility and clergy who feel their authority and special rights threatened will express their wishes to the king to have the gathering of representatives dissolved. The historic words of Mirabeau which were effective measures at the time "don't flinch until the bayonet is thrust upon you", truly brought us to a turning point in French as much as world history. From the National Consultative Assembly issued French independence and the aspirations of the Republic.

We do not want to specify that there is any clear similarity between pre-revolutionary France and Indonesia at this time. What is really true is that both contain many important economic and political similarities.

But in Indonesia it is not only the aristocracy that exploits, lives luxuriously, and doesn't pay tax, but also Dutch financial circles. That is why the situation here is excessive. While the money scattered around all over the place in Versailles still occasionally trickled down to the French people in various forms, of the money thrown around in Zandveert and Scheveningen, not one cent ever reaches the pockets of the *kromo* (small peasantry).

Under Governor General Dirk Fock and the Dutch capitalists based in Bogor, Indonesia faced financial bankruptcy. State finances in 1923 rose to a thousand million florins. Budget estimates for the year 1921 showed a deficit of 285,500,000. In other words the expenditure for the year 1921 showed a deficit amounting to 285,500,000 over returns. Like Necker[29] summoned by Louis XVI to improve the state finances, so Dirk Fock appeared in Indonesia to rescue the state finances from financial bankruptcy. Necker was incapable of doing anything because, until the end, the French nobility and clergy were stone-headed enough to hold onto their extraordinary economic and political rights. In the words of the Dutch villagers, pay tax even if the people are allowed to die from hunger.

Will Dirk Fock succeed in creating an exalted financial class to stand over the brown coloured (*berkulit sawo mateng*) people of Indonesia?

The earlier formulated plan to compel the sugar enterprises to guarantee better living and working conditions by expending some of the sugar capital was canceled after he arrived in Indonesia. When he wanted to impose taxes on oil there arrived the well-known threat from Colijn, "Lift this regulation or else we will be close down the oil wells".

Doctor Fock, obliged to nurse to health the otherwise sickly state finances, then turned to use a new instrument that even Necker lacked the courage to use.

The first stage was to enlarge the navy and police forces and to raise the wages of the high officials.

The second stage was to release the working class and decrease their wages, take back more from the suffering people and decrease the expenditure from people's schools and people's health.

Thus he calculated the balance of output and the imports can be improved.

Thus it was a measure exercised by a courageous state official otherwise usually exercised by political donkeys and sellers of nostrums at a time of hopelessness. How can the financial circles in Zorgvliet and Den Haag be satisfied with this? Variously, the imports and exports of such commodities as sugar, tea, matches, oil, and textiles, attract taxes, yet capital outlay can safely be recouped from the burden imposed upon the consumer, ie. by easily raising the prices of people's daily necessities. The government pawnshops and the salt monopoly adds to the heavy economic burden on the shoulders of the *kromo* until they are pushed beyond the limits of their capability. It is no exaggeration to say that an adult Javanese is burdened with one of the highest tax rates in the world. In the true sense of the word a Javanese owns nothing "except the air that he breathes".

Is there any hope that the economic crisis can be overcome? Certainly not as long thousands of rupiah as dividends yearly enter the pockets of the Dutch capitalists in Holland.

There is no other colonized land that is as financially drained as Indonesia, because in other colonized countries like Egypt, India, and the Philippines, or in semi-colonized countries like Persia, and China, inevitably part of the profits that remain in the pockets of the bourgeoisie will in whatever way be used domestically. Even if America or any other country is willing to lend millions of rupiah in capital to Indonesia, still the economic crisis cannot be overcome. Because millions of rupiah that have to be acquired annually are squeezed from the Indonesian working class as remittances abroad.

The economic future for the Indonesian people is even darker than that of the French people before 1789. Every Governor General sent to Bogor by the Dutch usurers, such as the case of Dirk Fock, was incapable of creating anything new except new taxes. There will not be a single Governor General capable of wiping out the deficit while the Dutch usurers seek dividends.

Because of this we are rapidly approaching a political crisis. The objective of all the conditions remains. The capability to organize ourselves, political morality, and absolute consciousness belongs to us alone.

But our path does not pass through parliament. That is precisely what happens in British India, Egypt, and the Philippines, where a strong native bourgeoisie is found, where the importance of their economy is the same as the imperialist economy and because of it political authority proceeds peacefully. Thus, although there is no certainty, national independence in India, and Egypt, will more or less proceed with the support of the masses via a "dominion" or national parliament. Our path is outside of parliament. Our path is through the politics of the Sarekat Sekerja.

The Indonesian National Assembly must be convened by ourselves and not with the consent of our enemies. The Indonesian National Assembly will undoubtedly be created at a time of violent physical, economic, or political clash like local revolt, general strike, and mass demonstrations. This will become the climax of all our labours. The creation of an Indonesian National Assembly is a life or death problem in our struggle for *merdeka* (freedom), a matter of "to be or not to be" in our fight against the holders of political and financial power.

This matter can be problematized if we are convinced that possible retaliatory measures by our enemies can be defended and crushed with success. This problem, if not confronted beforehand by convening the National

Consultative Council, will present the power holders with an ultimatum.

By convening the National Consultative Council we will demonstrate that the dominant powers that be are not capable of handling our problems, that we have confidence in wielding our own power, and that we can answer back to the retaliatory measures of our opponents successfully. Accordingly, we wish to govern our own domestic and external problems according to our own views and without the mediation of others, and that on this basis the power holders must give us our place. The Dutch administrative and technical cadre, both military and political, can continue to reside in Indonesia albeit under fixed conditions, so long as they are prepared to work under the new Indonesian administration.

It is certain that we cannot take this important decision if we are not supported by the whole Indonesian population. The PKI and Sarekat Rakyat has to be strengthened beforehand so that all sections along with the Sarekat Sekerja will truly constitute a militant force, prepared for our clarion call for action, and prepared to face the threat of machine guns and airplanes.

When Mirabeau uttered his courageous words, he actually knew that these words would reverberate among the extremely active workers in the towns facing Paris. If Louis XVI really used bayonets, he certainly would have been faced with a general revolt.

With the increasing suffering of the Indonesian people, mass economic and political actions can erupt at any time. If our economic and political organizations already attain the quality and quantity desired, if peasants, workers, traders, and students, really desire a new and better life and clearly promote themselves, only then can we convene the National Consultative Council of Indonesia. We must be convinced, if necessary to repeat "don't disperse, except at the end of a bayonet".

THUNDERBOLT TO CLEAN THE AIR

At the time of writing this brochure, comes a report that our party is threatened by "wild dogs". Peasants and unemployed are organized and dispatched to beat our members into line with sticks. Such officials that have already committed murder several times over are paid off and dispatched to make attempts on the lives of our responsible leaders. These demonstrations from the dregs of the Indonesian people are organized to create fear, to humble and to provoke our members. Now Injo [30] is the name of Indonesian fascism.

Mussolini, a man of absolute wickedness and reaction, inevitably creates revolutionary instruments according to one principle and principles for one political end. However, what principle does the Sarekat Injo hold to except desperation and debasement of character? Thus is the creation of a period of fascism.

You, the government, creators, givers of divine inspiration, intellectual planners, creators of this gloom! You think that your creations can crush us? Similarly, with prisons, exiles, blows with sticks, bullets, and other instruments from a dark world, your fascism will disappear like a snow drift in the rays of the sun.!!

But we do not hope for a utopia as if our road is short and smooth going. The land is dark, difficult, and full of poison, that is the road to independence. From left and right we have already heard the whispered messages of skeptical friends. How can we continue?

Heavy is the work of educating the masses who for centuries have experienced nothing else but humiliations and blows from sticks, from both our ruling class and a foreign ruling class, masses who are obliged to cringe and beg as if that was a normal thing are reduced to utopian thinking and slave mentality.

Heavy it appears to carry out its work of education under an authority not averse to untruths, violating laws which they make themselves, trampling on the rights of people, and crudely using instruments of violence, an authority with exceptional powers using modern instruments of repression on a compliant Asian people.

Heavy it seems to be to carry on the struggle

with an unarmed force, void of strength, and surrounded by traitors, waging a struggle against forces commanding gold, hirelings, and various other instruments of repression.

But truth is power, our truth is a struggle between those in authority and those subordinated, which is the dialectic of the growth of capitalism, is the stimulus in our revolutionary struggle, and the force which rises up (incites) and inspires to overthrow and give victory to the strong.

Suffering, still deeply endured, and increasingly ill-informed reaction, will strengthen our forces in short time and sap away at the enemy.

We call to the intellectual class!

Also your class will not be free from suffering. There will come a time when colonial capitalism, now able to use your energy will throw you away like a discarded fruit that has lost its sweetness. The capitalist disease, that is a crisis with no protection, will endure for a long time. You must also agitate like a thousand of your brothers in Japan and British India for the "intellectual proletarian class".

Haven't you heard the increasingly strident cry of the Indonesian masses for independence? Haven't you noticed that they are striding forward in the great struggle?

Will you delay even longer while

independence is seized by them so that they alone will taste the delicious fruits of victory. No, such a low and feeble response does not befit you. Because of it join yourselves into our force. But quickly, so that your class can also soon say with pride: "I will follow to help seize independence".

In the whirlwind of the coming revolution you will come to know the Indonesian masses in all their capabilities and weaknesses. There you will come to obtain an opportunity to use your moral and intellectual capability to launch the path of revolution. There you will become aware how delicious it is to carry our social work and to struggle for and with the masses. There you will understand the silence of life as an individual in a capitalist society.

If, in the near future, we can hold out hope for your help in towns and villages, on the beaches and extensive mountains of Indonesia, to rise up to claim rights and independence, then there is no enemy in the world capable of opposing the wave of the revolutionary typhoon.

In the atmosphere of an independent Indonesia, intellectual and social energy will blossom faster and better. Great wealth accumulated by the labour of Indonesians will remain in our country. Knowledge, otherwise controlled and distorted for the benefit of the Dutch capitalists, will soon blossom for the use and benefit of Indonesian society. Art and libraries will find new ground on which to take root. Even more certain, Indonesia will soon grow in the field of economics, intellect, and culture.

The time of hunger, suffering, and pariahs, such as the oppressed castes of India, belongs to a past dark century.

Fear of hunger, contagious diseases, and fear of extraction of taxes, police, and prison, also belongs to the past.

And the new era is breaking wherever the torch of communism will lead the young Indonesian people to a final direction: Independence, Culture, and Happiness for all Mankind.

China, April 1925

NOTES

1. Under the "ultra-conservative" governor generalship of Dirk Fock, along with his successors, De Graeff and De Jonge, and strongly supported by conservative Ministers of Colonies in The Hague, "a policy of repression toward the nationalist movement was inaugurated" (see. B. H. M. Vlekke, *Nusantara: A History of Indonesia*, V. Van Hoeve, The Hague, 1965, p.367.)

2. The actions by students in China in May 1925 include anti-Japanese boycotts led by students in Shanghai, and the strike-boycott by the All-China Federation of Trade Unions/Hong Kong Seaman's Union affecting a quarter of a million workers in the Canton delta, an important prelude to the Canton uprising of December 1927.

3. The Sarekat Rakyat (People's Union) emerged in February 1923 out of a split between the PKI and Sarekat Islam. At the end of 1924 the Party called for the Sarekat Rakyat, and its predominant peasant following, to liquidate itself and to concentrate all

work in the hands of the more revolutionary working classes.

4. Founded in Java in 1908, Budi Utomo was a pre-political organization catering to the sons of the lesser nobility.

5. Founded in 1911 by the radical Indo-European E.F.E. Douwes Dekker, the National Indische Partij proclaimed an "Indies" nationalism and called for independence. The government, however, refused recognition of the party and banished its leaders.

6. Indonesia's first mass organization, Sarekat Islam, was founded in 1912. While having its origins in Indonesian trader's solidarity vis-à-vis Chinese competition, it was only notionally Islamic from the start and, up until February 1923, entered into a relationship with the PKI.

7. A reference to the interests of the Morgan conglomerate in the US.

8. The Dawes Plan refers to the scheme whereby post-World War One Germany was obliged to transfer reparations to the European victors. In fact, these sums were then transferred to the US as loan repayments and interest, which, in turn, found their way back to Germany in the form of American investments. As two economic historians have written, "Germany exchanged her obligations under the Peace treaty for obligations to American investors". [See Sidney Pollard and Colin Holmes, *The End of the Old Europe, 1914-1939: Documents of European Economic History*, Edward Arnold, London, 1973, p.260] Following a review in 1924, an attempt was made to link reparations with Germany's

capacity to pay. Only the financial crisis of 1929 put a halt to this circular flow of payments.

9. Swaraj Party; the political movement in British India advocating self rule.

10. The so-called Ethical Policy with its concept of "Debt of Honour", represented, according to Legge, "an official attempt to foster as well as to control the direction of social change". See John Legge, *Indonesia,* Prentice-Hall, New Jersey, 1964, pp.8-9.

11. This is a reference to the Japan-USSR Treaty of 20 January 1925, inter alia, establishing diplomatic relations between the two countries and requiring Japan evacuate from the northern part of Sakhalin island.

12. The Diponegoro revolt, after Pangeran (Prince) Diponegoro (1785-1855), engaged the Dutch in central Java in the 1820s. an undisputed national hero against Dutch colonialism.

13. The Aceh revolt in this part of northern Sumatra took the form of a war against the Dutch in 1873-74. Still ongoing against rule by Jakarta, rebellions in Aceh are strongly founded in Islamic solidarity.

14. The Toli Toli revolt refers to the murder of a Dutch Controleur in north Sulawesi in May 1919 just after a speaking tour in the region by a leader of the Sarekat Islam.

15. The events of Priangan and Madiun are no doubt a reaction to the actions of the so-called Sarekat Hijau (Green Union) or gang members and thugs who, encouraged by the Dutch administration, attacked and intimidated PKI and Sarekat Islam

meetings, especially in Priangan.

16. Multatuli was the pseudonym of Eduard Douwes Dekker whose book, *Max Havelaari* was, in part, a criticism of Dutch colonial policy in literary form but also a satire of a "certain type of Dutch bourgeoisie" who blatantly ignored the conditions under which Indonesians toiled to produce their wealth (see Vlekke, *Nusantara: A History of Indonesia*... pp.303-05).

17. Hendrik Colijn was the Prime Minister of the Netherlands who had offered up a proposal, albeit rejected by the government, for a limited measure of self-government for the islands of Sumatra, Java, Borneo, and the eastern islands. A repatriate from Indonesia, Colijn held key position in successive cabinets between 1930 and 1941.

18. Loosely, *poenal sanctie* involved a labour contract penalty leading to arrest and prison and forced labour on plantations for violators.

19. This is a reference to the Volksraad or colonial parliament.

20. VSTP stands for the Railway and Train Labour Union.

21. Inlansche Verpendin; land tax for natives.

22. The economic centre is translated as Surakarta valley in chapter five of "Political note concerning the Indonesian Communist Party". See Harry J. Benda and Ruth J. McVey, *The Communist Uprisings of 1926-1927 in Indonesia*, Modern Indonesia Project, Southeast Asia Program, Cornell University, Ithaca, New York, 1960, pp.116.

23. The Djojo Bojo myth, given currency by the

Japanese occupation of the Dutch East Indies, held that the "*orang putih*" would be driven out by a yellow race.

24. Pasundan organization was formed in 1914 as a near counterpart to Budi Utomo, but for Sundanese. Jong Minahasa refers to the Young Minahasa Party of Sulawesi founded in 1918.

25. The Kanto earthquake of 1 September 1923 led to the deaths of an estimated 175,000 people in the Tokyo-Yokohama region and the destruction of two-thirds of the urban area.

26. The Singapore Naval base was voted by the short-lived Labour government of McDonald, which came to power in Britain in 1924 as a way of getting around the terms of the Washington Agreement preventing the concerned powers from building up a Far Eastern fleet. Construction proceeded slowly under the Conservative government, was suspended by the incoming Labour government in 1929, but accelerated as the danger from Japan increased, especially with the Japanese occupation of Manchuria, and withdrawal from the League of Nations the following year. See C. M. Turnbull, *A History of Singapore, 1819-1975*, Oxford University Press, Kuala Lumpur, 1977, p.163.

27. Correctly, Takekoshi Yosaburō (1865-1950) was a Japanese politician-historian and a committed advocate of Japanese expansion in the South Seas, rather than China.

28. Jean le Rond d'Alembert (1717-1783) was a eminent Parisian mathematician and philosopher, author, inter alia, of *Precision of the Equinoxes*.

29. Jacques Necker was French minister

responsible for economic reforms in the 1770s.

30. This is a reference to the Sarekat Hijau, elements opposed to the pro-communist forces.

ABOUT THE AUTHOR

Geoffrey C. Gunn is the author of a number of cognate works on revolution in Laos, Vietnam, and Cambodia. He has held teaching positions in schools and universities in Australia, Laos, Libya, Brunei Darussalam, Singapore, Japan (Nagasaki) and, Macau, China. In 2000, he served in the United Nations mission in East Timor, returning in 2003 as an adviser to the Timor-Leste "Truth Commission."

He first visited Indonesia in 1967, then a student of Indonesian history and language at Melbourne University, Australia. Further detail on the life and times of Tan Malaka is examined in the author's *Singapore and the Asian Revolutions* (Macau, 2008). He is also the author of a work on Brunei-Malay language, namely, *Language, Power and Ideology in Brunei Darussalam* (Ohio University Press, 1987). His most recent work is *Rice Wars in Colonial Vietnam: The Great Famine and the Viet Minh Road to Power* (Rowman & Littlefield, 2014).

Tan Malaka Naar de 'Republiek Indonesia'

Geoffrey C. Gunn

www.ingramcontent.com/pod-product-compliance
Lightning Source LLC
Chambersburg PA
CBHW020930090426
42736CB00010B/1098